Living Shamanism

Unveiling the Mystery

T0095888

Living Shamanism

Unveiling the Mystery

Julie Dollman

MOON
BOOKS

Winchester, UK
Washington, USA

First published by Moon Books, 2013
Moon Books is an imprint of John Hunt Publishing Ltd., Laurel House, Station Approach,
Alresford, Hants, SO24 9JH, UK
office1@jhpbooks.net
www.johnhuntpublishing.com
www.moon-books.net

For distributor details and how to order please visit the 'Ordering' section on our website.

Text copyright: Julie Dollman 2012

ISBN: 978 1 78099 732 2

All rights reserved. Except for brief quotations in critical articles or reviews, no part of this
book may be reproduced in any manner without prior written permission from the publishers.

The rights of Julie Dollman as author have been asserted in accordance with the Copyright,
Designs and Patents Act 1988.

A CIP catalogue record for this book is available from the British Library.

Design: Stuart Davies

Printed and bound by CPI Group (UK) Ltd, Croydon, CR0 4YY

We operate a distinctive and ethical publishing philosophy in all
areas of our business, from our global network of authors to
production and worldwide distribution.

CONTENTS

Acknowledgments

It is important to honour and remember the people who have been instrumental in being supportive, or those who have played a specific role during the time of the book's journey from conception to birth.

I would like to make a heartfelt mention and show my gratitude to all of those dear souls who helped me.

To my husband Paul and daughters Ella & Kate. It is very rare for such special souls to incarnate together and for those souls to love and support each other as you all do. I am always in awe of your wisdom and openness to the life that we are now part of.

To Eddie O'Hanlon, thank-you from the bottom of my heart for joining me on this journey; I am very grateful for your knowledge of the English language and for being so enthusiastic when working on this book.

To Barry Murphy, I do not think you know how generous you were while we stayed with you on the Farm. If it were not for your gracious acceptance of our need to find peace... this book may never have been conceived.

Last but not least I would like to thank the generosity of our dear friends, Catherine Maguire and Vincent McMahon; for the ability of being able to live within our hearts as an extended shamanic family; and for the joyous exchange of communication and discussion as we all explore the ether together in our quest for information and answers.

Introduction

When people meet in normal society it is not unusual for a conversation to include the question, 'what is it that you do?' When someone asks me that question, I proudly reply, 'I am a Shamanic practitioner'. More often than not my reply is often met by either a puzzled look, or a further question along the lines of 'what is that?' I then muster up an array of sentences and well chosen words to explain the wondrous and extensive role of a Shaman.

Unfortunately the English language is somewhat limited when one tries to find the words to explain something that is really, in its purest essence and methodology, quite mysterious!

At times it is not unusual for me to reflect over the past seven years, and wonder how on earth my life changed so drastically, and I often ask myself this...

How does one go from being so immersed in a world of commercialism, power and 'wants', to becoming a 'Shaman'?

When I was in my mid-40s and working as a criminal analyst I lived in suburbia in Buckinghamshire with my husband and two children. We lived as many other people of our generation do, having a mortgage and paying the bills. We socialised, worked very hard, gave dinner parties and I loved shopping for all the creature comforts until one transformational day in March 2002. My husband and I attended a talk in London given by an American anthropologist Dr Alberto Villoldo, who for the last 20 years had been working with and tutored by Peruvian medicine men (descendents of the Inca). He enjoyed a unique life of adventure which came with the privilege of being taught some wonderful ancient teachings.

On that cold, dark night we left work and travelled the 30 odd miles into the centre of London to the eclectic St James' Church Piccadilly, known as 'Alternatives'...

*In 1982 the Rev Donald Reeves was invited to be the Rector of St James Church. From the word go he saw the church as a place of light and hope for London. To Donald this meant creating a space for debate and acceptance. Under this belief Turning Points was born. Turning Points evolved into **Alternatives** a few years later.*

The demonstrations he gave were quite unfathomable and amazing. He showed the spellbound audience just how much influence our bad experiences, ancestral issues and traumas have on our energy bodies; and subsequently our physical health. The inferences he made were literally astounding. When he spoke my husband and I sat there captivated. He wasn't giving a sales pitch, he was opening our senses to a completely unknown and new world, and when the penny dropped as they say, we felt we had been transported straight into the realms of Bilbo Baggins and the Hobbits!

Within a month we signed up for a two-year course to learn the ways of the Peruvian Shaman and how to 'heal the light body' (the light body is a term used to describe the body of energy (or aura) that surrounds the physical body).

Several years later, now in my early 50s, I am living in rural Ireland with my husband, family and dogs. We provide healing for those who come, we grow vegetables, we attend fire ceremonies, but, most importantly, we have learnt the true meaning of 'living in right relationship'.

Right relationship is a term we use when we talk about a journey of realisation and actualisation of the self. It is a journey into learning and understanding about establishing a harmonious and balanced relationship within your own energy bodies. Right relationship is achieved when you are in a balanced relationship with the Earth, other people, yourself and nature, the 'whole'.

When I first started to write this book it was entitled 'Forgive my Humanness'. I wanted to share with you my own journey into Shamanism, and that was exactly how I wrote the first, second and third drafts... until a wise women and fellow Shaman said to me: 'Why don't you write a book that de-mystifies Shamanism?'

To be honest, when she first suggested it, I was completely bemused. The initial book, I believed, was written and based around the fact that I wanted to show the world how a relatively normal individual (one devoid of exceptional genetics and lived life without experiencing any real traumas or outstanding experiences) ended up as a Shamanic healer. I wanted so much to tell the story of how I immersed myself in an unsatisfying life which revolved around work, socialising and spending money, to then living life as a Shaman who could scale the underworld and retrieve a soul part that had been lost by a person during a heinous life experience.

On reflection and in the absence of my ego, I believe that my initial writing and stories had sped into overdrive. The words spewed from me in a fervent need to openly share my life story in order to hit home the most basic of spiritual facts : that *anyone* could find a spiritual path and have a spiritual tool box that would accompany them whilst dealing with life's tricky curve balls. In truth I now see the initial drafts of Forgive My Humanness as a cathartic self healing. It was a need to recapitulate my own journey so that I could happily lay the stories of the past in the past, allowing my spirit to fly free and my soul to realign to a predetermined destiny.

'Living Shamanism' is a book that examines Shamanism from a Western perspective. It does this by strolling through the history of Shamanism from a cultural point of view. It then takes you on a journey to establish the ways of indigenous peoples, old cultures and mainstream religions, before moving into the present, determining exactly what it is that many modern day people have forgotten. What is the true meaning of relationship;

relationship to the self, others, the Earth and the Cosmos?

This book looks at the possible causes of our disconnection from our ability to experience authentic relationships and many other everyday issues, and it does this in a frank and honest way. I use some of my own life experiences that I happen to know are the experiences of many others too. These experiences illustrate how easy it is to get seduced into a world of illusion and, more importantly, how easy it is to get the help you need simply by taking responsibility for yourself; acknowledging the sacred in all life, and using some of the many tools we use and have collected over the years.

My own experience and journey into Shamanism was, at times, like being on a white knuckle ride that sometimes propelled me uncontrollably into the unknown; an amazing journey into the wonderment of mystery.

Demystifying Shamanism to me is like proving to you that a magic trick really is magical after all! For me, the acknowledgement of my own awakening and appreciation of how my so-called fulfilled, evolved and material lifestyle left so many voids. It also left an emptiness in the pit of my stomach that could not be sated... until that is, the day I slowly began to walk the path of a medicine woman.

Even though I follow a Shamanic lifestyle, I am very aware that there are many spiritual paths that one can pursue today. Most of them require us to take personal responsibility and show up as agents of change, especially now in this current collective consciousness of global dis-harmony. Whether one chooses a dogmatic, religious or flexible exploration into the self, that choice and experience is completely yours to make.

For many of us, our first experience of a spiritual path is usually linked to an organised religious faith; maybe Eastern Christianity, Catholicism, Protestantism, Islam, Judaism, etc. Quite often, our first experience is derived from adopting our parents' belief system, or maybe a religion promulgated by our school.

As we get older more often than not this happens in our 40s, some of us start to question mainstream religions and their ethics, if only to satisfy our ability of freedom of choice and free will.

For me, after a great deal of soul searching, the path I chose was a Shamanic one. I found that the ancient teachings I had learnt from the honourable and impeccable Qero tribes had afforded me my own personal key; one that would unlock the door so to speak. It would help me do this by not only allowing me travel to other dimensions that were light-years away from my present world of illusion, but also by providing me with many answers to help fill those uncomfortable periods of emptiness that I was experiencing.

The answers I was given help to bestow on me a much deeper sense of one-ness and relationship. I feel such deep gratitude and reconnection to the Earth and the people that I share my life with, and with those who come to me for healing. In fact, so much so, that often the sheer wonderment of it all literally wants to burst out of my heart centre!

'Living Shamanism' has been written to illustrate certain aspects where I wish I could have used these words: 'Please forgive my human bullishness, arrogance and ignorance'!

I want to share with you how I had become wrapped up a world which measures its people by how much we succeed, and create an unsustainable and somewhat insurmountable ideal of a lifestyle. It is a lifestyle that often damages us and others, purely created by a sheer need to make something of ourselves. I want to show just how fearful, aggressive and violent many have become as a race; so much so that we are now a race that seems impotent and defensive. So often in our lives we combat this by abusing our power; whether that is a power over others or a power that boldly strips another's beliefs or culture away; perhaps all due to the fact what we do not understand makes us fearful. It is very much a Catch 22 scenario!

'Living Shamanism' is for any person who wishes to awaken themselves to the possibility of a more harmonious way of living. It will take you on a journey, some of which will be that of discovery accompanied by my own experience. Other parts will be an awakening and awareness to certain levels of our collective human hostility, for example Integrity; Void Fillers; Relationships; the Masculine and Feminine; our limitations of Old Belief Systems and Death, and much more.

I will delve into that old adage of our expectations of Love; the many roles we have adopted for ourselves; our need to be in control or be controlling. The book will also delve into the alchemical process of re-inventing the self through a metamorphic process from seed (birth), germination (life experiences), to the ultimate goal of illumination (wisdom and intelligence).

Lastly, and just as importantly, I want to *de-mystify* the ethos around 'Ceremony', as this under-used practice is often a missing piece of the jigsaw when attempting to attain an 'authentic relationship' with ourselves, others and the world that we live in.

Throughout the book I will intersperse stories and exercises to offer you some healing, personal work and ways to help re-programme your power of thought, feelings and emotions. Hopefully, it will go a long way in helping to de-mystify Shamanism for you.

NO... Shamans DO NOT all run around banging drums and shaking rattles whilst wearing long feathered cloaks with animal bones around their necks!

Some of us actually do dress in a westernised way; wear make-up and dye our hair to cover the greys! Many still buy toiletries and cleaning items that may or may not be environmentally friendly; and yes, some even use a microwave!

However, what we may do is stand around a fire to mulch

away our human toxic issues. We may sit with our backs up against an old ancient tree. We communicate with nature, and we journey to the stars and other dimensions and realms. You will find some of us who can vision the future, or channel other more evolved beings. I guess if all of that makes us crazy or weird well then we stand before you both guilty and naked; naked to the possibility of actually enjoying this wondrous journey into the great and magical mystery.

I hope you enjoy the book and find something that resonates, or an exercise that will help you through a tough time. If not, to quote another Western Shaman; 'This book will make great fuel for the fire!'

Chapter 1

What is a Shaman?

Shamanism is not a faith, but a wisdom tradition in which we learn purely from our own individual, collective and personal experience. It is not a religion and is dogma-free; indeed it supports any existing spiritual practice one already has. Many of us deeply desire a connection to our own 'soulfulness' and that of all other living beings in a free and natural way. This is the essence of Shamanism.
John Cantwell
Slí an Chroí (Pathway of the Heart)

To firstly understand what a Shaman is, or indeed the role played in the present and in the past, I would like to take you on a chronological explanation of where the term *Shaman* comes from and why so many of us so-called Western humans are called to follow the path of our hearts.

For many of us it is *not* all about moving into seclusion away from the madness of cities; dressing anyway we choose. Nor is it about conducting strange or closeted rituals; or a wish to be labelled by the rest of society as weird or strange! For many it is so much more. We simply and willingly wish to enter into a more sacred connection to 'Gaia' and explore deeper levels in order to heal ourselves and others.

For many people who take their first steps into Shamanism, it is very often an attempt to try to heal their own wounds by understanding their lives and healing their life experiences; turning that knowledge into wisdom and intelligence, so that they understand what pushes their buttons. This often entails a journey into a hidden arena of the dark, an area which hides away a repressed self so that when they bring light to those dark experiences they no longer cause us hurt and pain. Today Western Shamanism is often referred to as: 'The Path of the Wounded Healer'.

Thousands of years ago medicine men and women discovered how to maximise the human abilities of mind and spirit for the purpose of healing and problem-solving. Shamanism is a way of life that embraces the principle of one-ness with all things, the web of life and nature. A Shaman can become at one with the rivers and oceans; feel life in the earth or a tree and feel the heartbeat in stones and mountains. They can also call on the ancestors for guidance. A Shaman can travel through the thin veils to other dimensions solely for the purpose of wisdom and to attain healing for another. A Shaman also acknowledges that a harsh word or incident can have the same effect as a ripple in the water... and its consequence can affect seven generations!

A History of the Indigenous Role of Shaman

The history books say that it is possible that Shamanic practices originate as far back as the Palaeolithic periods and certainly as early as the Neolithic period, predating all organised and dogmatic religions. Most Shamanic knowledge was never written down and was only passed on orally; therefore it is difficult to formally pinpoint a specific date of origin.

I would suspect that practices date back much further than man's recorded knowledge of history.

Maybe you subscribe to Darwin's theory that all life is related to a common ancestor such as a fish, bird or mammal. Darwin states that these creatures evolved naturally over time using natural selection. Or do you subscribe to the Bible's account which reads: 'In the beginning God created the heavens and Earth in seven days'? Maybe you hold a different belief, for example, one where visitors came from other planets and mixed their DNA with ours, so that humans would evolve quicker.

Whichever theory feels right in your heart, my belief is that Shamans have been around for thousands of years, it is only the title that changes.

Shamanism had a strong tradition in Europe before the rise of monotheism (a belief in one god) and it remains a traditional, organised religion in Eastern and Northern Europe, and some provinces of Russia and Siberia.

In Asia the word 'Wu' meaning Shaman or spirit healer first appeared in the late Shang Dynasty (1600-1046 BCE) and was also mentioned later (1045-256 BCE). There are recorded details about male and female Shamans who would serve as exorcists, healers, rainmakers, soothsayers etc. Shamanic practices continue in present-day Chinese culture. In Korea, Shamans are consulted for financial and marital decisions, although only female Shamans, known as Mudangs, take on this role. Shamanism is part of the native Japanese religion called Shinto. Today Shinto has merged with Buddhism and other Japanese folk culture. There are also strong Shamanistic influences in Tibetan Buddhism; when Buddhism became popular with Shamanic peoples such as the Tibetans, Mongols and Manchi beginning in the 8th Century.

In Vietnam, Shamans conduct rituals in many of the religious traditions that co-mingle in the majority and minority populations. In their rituals, such as music and dance, special garments are worn, and offerings are made as part of the performance that surrounds the spirit journey.

There are many Eskimo groups who cover a large area stretching from Eastern Siberia through Alaska and Northern Canada to Greenland, where Shamanistic practices and beliefs have been recorded in several parts of this large area.

Some forms of African traditional religion are also included as Shamanistic; especially the Dogon Sorcerers, who indulge in communication with a deity called Ama, who advises them on both healing and divination. However, in the 9th Century healers in Africa were often referred to as witch doctors that practiced

Juju.

Most famously in North America and in other First Nations, cultures have had diverse religious beliefs and there was never just one universal native American religion or spiritual system. It is known that many had traditional healers, mystics, and medicine people, though none of them used the term Shaman to describe these roles. More commonly the roles were described as tribal, Shamanic or totemic faiths.

Not all indigenous communities have roles for specific individuals who mediate with the spirit world on behalf of their community. Among those that have this sort of religious structure, spiritual methods and beliefs may have some commonalities, though many of these commonalities are due to some nations being closely related, or coming from the same region. With the arrival of European settlers, the practice of 'Shamanism' was discouraged.

In South America, however, Shamanic healing is found amongst many indigenous peoples, especially in Panama, Peru, Brazil, and Ecuador; using a variety of practices including making sacred talismans, rituals and ayahuasca (a psychedelic herbal potion used for physical and psychological healing), used for dreaming and healing.

In the Peruvian rainforest, the Amazonian Shamans conduct healing on altars known as mesas. High up in the Andes their Qero brothers carry a portable 'mesa' around with them, which comprises a symbolically woven cloth that holds many medicine articles and artefacts. *The symbols depicted in these cloths are meant to date back 1000s of years.*

Moving down to Papua New Guinea, indigenous tribes believe that illness is caused by dark spirits that cling to a person's body and literally poison them. Shamans in that region will purge the dark spirits from a person.

In Australia various aboriginal groups refer to their Shamans as 'clever men and women', who use a material called Mahan

---

which they believe will give them magical powers. Besides healing and having contact with spiritual beings, they are involved in secret initiations and other ceremonies.

There is an early English name for Shaman and it is Seidr (pronounced seethe). This is an Old Norse term for a 'type of sorcery or witchcraft'. Seidr has links to Old Germanic customs. Seidr means cord or string, although it involved spinning charms. They also used the Runes as a way of divination. There is a reference to Seidr in the Sami tribes in Finland, Sweden and Norway.

There is an assumption that the ancient religious practices of the peoples of the British Isles and Ireland mirror those of contemporary Nnative peoples of America and Australia. This also underlies the popularity of Celtic Shamanism and the fact that Shamanism is the most ancient and universal form of religious behaviour. This subsequently leads to the identification of Shamanistic elements in early Irish tales such as Buile Suibhne (a legendary King of Ulster) and the stories of Finn MacCool (a mythical hunter warrior). Thus myth and legend are interpreted as evidence that contemporary Celtic Shamanism is revitalising an ancient spiritual discipline, rather than existing as historical or archaeological evidence.

How do you become a Shaman?

Certainly in indigenous cultures around the world, both now and in the past, the role of Shaman is a calling. Some individuals who are called typically experience an illness of some sort over a prolonged period of time. This illness will prompt the individual to seek out spiritual guidance and other Shamanic healers. Such illnesses are usually not healed by doctors or Western medicine.

The Shaman heals through spiritual means that consequently affect the human world by bringing about restored health. For others the role of Shaman is passed on from father to son or mother to daughter orally. Subjects undergo initiation to awaken the codes of light from within.

The Qero Shamans, who I studied with, are typically selected by spirit to undertake the calling by being struck by lightning! (They live high up in the Andes and this is a measured method of pre-selection). Today, the calling of a typical Western Shaman usually occurs after a person has sought out ways to heal themselves due to recurring bad life experiences. This is where the term 'wounded healer' (the archetypal name for the Shaman's journey) comes from.

It is imperative for anyone (whether indigenous or Western), when undertaking the calling of the Shaman, that they first take on the responsibility of healing their own wounds before becoming a practicing Shamanic healer or seer. Humans need to taste that dark place of being on the brink of collapse; whether that is metaphorical or physical; and to know how to recover from that dark place by means of gaining the knowledge and power to heal. The Shaman, more often than not, must become sick or wounded to understand this.

Shamans gain knowledge and the power to heal by entering into the spiritual world or other dimensions. The Shaman may have or acquire spirit guides in the spirit world, who often guide and direct the Shaman in his or her travels. These spirit guides are always present within the Shaman, although some only encounter them when entering a trance. The spirit guide energizes the Shaman, enabling him/her to enter the spiritual dimension. The Shaman heals within the spiritual dimension by returning lost parts of the human soul from wherever they have gone. The Shaman also cleanses excess negative energies which confuse or pollute the soul.

Shamans & Religion

By now we realise that the word Shaman or Shamanism is a basic anthropological term to determine a range of beliefs and practices that involve communication with the spiritual world.

By this sentence alone we can assume how one could easily see this as an amazing power. In the eyes of dogmatic religions this is a power that really should not be available for any man or women, unless they are representative of the one true God!

Over time there has been so much documented history showing recorded instances where these representatives of God have misconstrued the gifts of medicine men and women (who acted as healers in their communities) as those who dabbled in the black arts and were in cahoots with Satan himself. Persecution, murder, torture and elimination followed swiftly and one of the earliest recorded punishments of a witch happened in England in the 10th Century. The most famous of these curtailments of the feminine is the well-documented 'Witch Trials' which spread throughout England, Europe and the Americas in the 16th Century.

Of course it would be naive to state that all Shamans and those who use magic as their art are innocent. Where there are those whose purpose is to help others, of course there is a polar opposite whereby some only serve to create chaos, mayhem and use these gifts for personal gain.

Why is it that Shamanism in many indigenous cultures is in decline? There are two answers to this. The first is that Shamans who are well versed in the practice of ritual, journey and healing techniques are growing old and quite simply do not have anyone to pass their knowledge on to; bearing in mind that even now much of that knowledge is still in oral form.

Many children who grow up within these cultures see a much more evolved and materialistic lifestyle to be had outside of their villages. Many head off into the bright lights of the metropolis to better their lives! The result is that the old ways of wisdom and knowledge eventually die out.

The second reason may well be more obvious. It involves the spread of organised religions and doctrines. These particular factions first sent out their missionaries around 1598; the Jesuits first sent out their emissaries in order to spread the word of God...

> 'He said therefore to them again: Peace be to you. As the Father hath sent me, I also send you.' (John 20:21)
> 'And he said to them: The harvest indeed is great, but the labourers are few. Pray ye therefore the Lord of the harvest, that he send labourers into his harvest.
> Go: Behold I send you as lambs among wolves.'
> (Luke 10:2–3).

Clearly at that time it was important that these religions brought people into their churches, thus ensuring that the old pagan beliefs were vanquished; ending old superstitions, magic and non-formalised ritual. (Bear in mind that the heads of religion often needed and wanted to have power over these unruly heathens).

Is Shamanism in decline? Well, what is strange is that the indigenous Shamanic healers (who acted as mediators, healers and seers in the past) are dying out. There is now a huge incline in interest in the West to reignite the old traditions and belief systems of our ancestors! There are many thousands of Westerners who now undertake courses and teachings in order to revive what was lost, in a fervent desire to live in authentic relationship! The illusion is finally cracking and many people are starting to see through the lies and deceit that are often illustrated or portrayed by their governments, banks and pharmaceutical organisations.

Many people are yearning for a freer life, to break free from the jails that have been placed around them by continual and relentless statutes and laws.

Many, many people now yearn to be in a truly authentic relationship with themselves, others, their Earth and the cosmos.

Chapter 2

Shamanism versus Religion

Shamanism over the centuries has been viewed by mainstream religions, among others, as a weird and wonderful practice. Although its origins may be ancient, it far exceeds its evolution. It is both mythical and transformational; even more than that, it transcends far beyond the physical; way out into the ether and into the mystical.

What is the difference between indigenous peoples and their beliefs and the old religions and the mainstream religions that we now know?

After all, there is one basic fundamental similarity isn't there? And that is faith! This is possibly the one thing that everyone who states what religion they believe in must have and hold. So the glue that unites humans is the ability to have faith in something. I would like to add another comparable requirement and that is love. For whatever belief one has, then surely holding love deep in their hearts and openly showing love to another must also be crucial?

Therefore, if the basis of religion is faith and love, then how on earth can we quantify thousands of religious wars, terrorist acts, ethnic cleansings, murders, casting out of the flock, and the pitting of one neighbour against the other? What is the common ingredient at play here? After all, if religion has the basis of love and faith in a divine being, then surely that is not the source of the problem, is it? Of course not; the base line ingredient here is man or human-being! And to further this, it all boils down to a need for power.

The word **religion** is defined as:

...a cultural system that creates powerful and long-lasting meaning by establishing symbols that relate humanity to beliefs and values. Many religions have narratives, symbols, traditions and sacred histories that are intended to give meaning to life or to explain the origin of life or the universe. They tend to derive morality, ethics, religious laws or a preferred lifestyle from their ideas about the cosmos and human nature...

If *that* is the definition of religion, why on earth did it all become so problematic? I think we all know the answer to that: it was when *Man* became involved. Quite simply, inside each human being are many facets; but in *all* of us lie some of the same. One of those is fear, and the other is power. To whatever degree it is within you (whether you are the bravest warrior or an ignorant bully) as soon as life or the self is threatened with extinction or danger, then you will see *both* of those words come out to play. When a human is faced with the fear of extinction that is when the overriding need to survive and overthrow become the main criteria. Looking at the many religious wars alone, all fought in the name of their god, is surely enough proof.

Even if you look at the history of the early civilisations, whether they were Sumerian (an early civilisation from Mesopotamia (5300- 4100 BC); or Minoan from Crete (3500- 2600 BC); the Celtic peoples from Middle Europe, France, Britain, Wales, Scotland and Ireland (800-450 BC); or the Egyptian Civilisations (5500 BC); they all mention a lengthy history of battles. Man has been fighting Man for as long as history can qualify the data. Warring with others may have less to do with religion and much more to do with power.

It is safe to say that it is the need for power and domination that is the primary downfall of humans. A difference in belief and religion is just an excuse. Therefore, why is it that humans need to be powerful? Surely if you take that need away you would be left with a peaceful Earth?

There is one unusual and very controversial train of thought from a Dr Michael Salla (an Exo-Scientist from a University in Washington, USA) that states that Earth and its inhabitants are an elaborate alien experiment!

Dr Salla states:

Manipulative ET groups provided Earth humans with advanced technology to further instil an agenda of control against willing Earth elites who were indoctrinated by 'Alien Gods'. The creation of technology would also be used to inspire the creation of weapons of war, in which wars would be waged in the name of defending 'religious' systems, in turn guided by Extraterrestrial gods who sought us to 'divide and rule'. (Canadian National Newspaper)

Examining historic accounts from the Hopi Indians, Egyptians, Maya, Aztec and many other ancient civilisations, all of them mention strange phenomenon that came from the sky, just like our modern day UFOs. Most of these ancient civilisations had beliefs in gods that had either interacted with them or created them.

These gods would teach them, guide them and rule over them with supernatural powers. Some people today regard these beliefs, held by these ancient civilisations, as simply myths or legends. If it was true that the gods were really advanced beings, wouldn't it help to explain the advancements in education and technology that these gods had made possible; advancements that were required to build those amazing structures built by ancient civilisations?

Today, ancient sites like the Nazca Lines, Egyptian Pyramids and Mayan Pyramids, do tend, in some curious way, to point to the existence of ancient aliens. Maybe, just maybe, the answer to our future is opening our minds to the possibilities of our past? Just something for you to ponder on!

Even though many people do agree with these articles and

statements (and yes it does provide us with a possible hypothesis as to why humans are incredibly power crazy and have the need to dominate cultures and nations that they simply do not understand), we all need to keep an open mind on this possibility until evidence emerges to prove it one way or another.

Therefore, the next point for thought should be: as religion has become so lost in its own need for power and domination, on a far greater scale, we seem to have lost the fundamental basis of it. Is that basis *faith* and *love*?

Religion, in its authentic role, the ritual, the sanctuary it provides and allowing people to have faith and a place to find peace and to pray, is a wonderful institution. There is nothing that can beat going into a church and sitting quietly with your thoughts, or meditating in such a sacred space, in order to find peace and solace. There is nothing wrong with attending an uplifting service, singing from your heart and praying as a community.

However, there is a flaw in the way that some men and women of the cloth find that the only way to pass on the word of God is by using fierce preaching; calling their parishioners sinners and using fear as a way to drive the message home. This is where their roles and functions go awry. Religion seems to be fearful of man's ability to take responsibility for a spiritual path; after all, surely we would all evolve much better if we were allowed to talk directly to the Divine. Here again, religion has form for being subversive and dangerous; the stories of the past; religious wars; the constant need to control man is where the darkness lies; flawed human beings taking advantage of the weak. Once again, what does it all boil down to; human beings, flawed and weak, who have taken the gift and abused their positions?

What is the reason so many Western individuals are turning their backs on organised religion and places of worship?

A Eurobarometer poll taken in 2005 found that out of 25 EU

member states, an average of 18% stated: 'I do not believe there is any sort of spirit, god or life force'. The member states with the highest numbers included Germany 25%, Belgium & the Netherlands 27%, and Czech Republic 30%.

A Gallup Poll taken in Europe during the period April 2007 to April 2008, asked: 'Does religion occupy an important place in your life?' 'A percentage of 50% from 24 out of 42 European countries answered: 'No, religion does not occupy an important place in our lives'. This is quite amazing, especially regarding the history of domination that the main religions of Eastern Christianity, Catholicism, Judaism, Islam and Protestantism have held in the past.

According to sources, the change towards atheism started at the turn of the 20th Century. The belief that an individual's ability to choose and exercise their own free will became much more important and suddenly changed the churches' hold over individuals. It was possibly due to the constant scolding and threatening of fear, damnation, excommunication and the inability to attain martyrdom. It is true that all of us, who have any experience of religion, remember those terrifying words about being 'placed before your god to account for your sins on judgement day!' Maybe that threat alone was enough for many to exercise their own free will?

Free will is the freedom to choose a route towards a particular outcome, although that route is not measured or assured. Free Will is not the same as absolute freedom of choice. Free will does, however, depend on personal needs and circumstances.

Therefore, what we do have is the ability to choose compassionate action. This could be why mainstream religions are losing their grip on humanity. As humans evolve and rationalise, their innate spiritual and intelligent minds are starting to see through the religious statutes as we start to ask ourselves whether the power of religion, coupled with the doctrine, actually makes sense to many of us. When things do not make sense, we have to find something that does, or we completely disown it. When we have a bad experience, or we lose someone, we start to question the existence of a kind, benevolent and forgiving God. We look to blame someone or something for making us go through that experience or loss. More often than not, it is our faith in something that is the first to be blamed.

However, what we often neglect to consider is the old adage of cause and effect.

Cause and effect is the relationship between any event or experience, the 'cause', and the subsequent event or experience, known as the 'effect'. (Types of causes include: objects, processes, properties, facts and states of affairs).

The principle of cause and effect does not include the axiom of chance, as this is determined as a cause that has not happened or become recognised yet. Humans happily ignore *their* part in any given event or experience, since if we became aware of it we could happily take ownership of the part we have played in it. It seems much easier to blame our faith or God figurehead rather than take personal responsibility for creating a cause or effect or both!

The negative experiences, wounds and events we encounter in our lives are often enough to detour us away from any kind of faith or belief, as the effect of enduring such a bad experience places many humans in the state of a wounded victim. The more we stay in this wounded place the more negativity and toxic experiences we draw to ourselves. This is the law of attraction.

Therefore, the more we suffer, the more we suffer! It is like a perpetual circle where we stay, just like the Catholic concept of purgatory. We will stay there until we either seek help, healing or have an epiphany. Only then will we start to clear away that toxic sludge and hopefully start to attract the light back into our lives.

There is a detrimental side, however, to disowning any kind of faith (faith does not have to be attached to a mainstream religion either). When this occurs, where do we humans go to get help? Where do we turn when things are really tough, especially in the absence of a trusted friend or belief system?

Most are instinctive in a need to connect to something that is either divine or natural in order to pull ourselves back from that dark recess. Alternatively, we may look for external means to fill and sate the void that has been caused by an absence of faith or belief.

The beginning of a disconnection starts right there. It begins with pulling away from a known and personal belief in *something*. In turn, it may then leave us 'outside in the cold', floundering alone with our thoughts and emotions. We may then become people looking to fill and satisfy our inner voids because we feel so disconnected.

The Bible sought to punish us as it taught that we 'had to account for our sins', just as Adam and Eve were punished and kicked out of the Garden of Eden because they disobeyed God, subsequently frightening every Adam and Eve from that moment on. This is a religious slant I do not believe in.

When we lose our personal beliefs and faith in whatever we have chosen, metaphorically we do the same thing to ourselves. We cast ourselves out into the shadows and into the wilderness. Many humans are ill equipped to cope with being in that place, as we live in the Western world of plenty and availability. We seek refuge in the need to satisfy our sorrows; fill our aching hearts and stomachs with whatever substance or void filler we can get our hands on; all in the need to feel better about ourselves.

Usually, if we do not look for external vices, then we will turn it inwards, as our powerful thoughts and emotions eat away at our bodies or minds until one or the other fails and becomes sick in the process.

What do Shamans believe in?

It is difficult to specifically define Shamanic belief. The term 'Shaman' encompasses a vast range of techniques, rather than just subscribing to any one belief system.

For example, you will discover that many Western Shamans embrace varying beliefs that include mainstream religions, Buddhism, Hinduism, or even a belief in the Fairy Folk. The term 'Shaman' is something we do, rather than just being another term for a religious belief system.

Shamans do, however, believe in subtle energy, and we believe in two specific types of this: Heavy Energy (Hucha) and Light Energy (Sami).

(The words Hucha and Sami are terms used by Peruvian Shamans, who use Quechua as their main language)

A Shaman will embrace anything and everything. We are taught to release the roles we assume and the old belief systems of others that may bind us. The one criterion is that we should *not* judge, collude, engage or criticise. Most importantly, we must arrive fresh for every experience.

To describe a Shamanic belief is best illustrated like this: A great many religious people will happily pray, worship and look up to the sky in order to vocalise their beliefs. While doing this, they are very content in praying to something they cannot see or physically hold!

A Shaman will also pray. It is what we have been doing for thousands of years, long before the onslaught of any dogmatic religion.

The slight difference in the way we pray is this, when we want to communicate with spirit, source or the Divine, we close our eyes, open our heart centres and journey to the space

23

between spaces and have a conversation in the light. We do not look at God as an external being or separatist; on the contrary we see the Divine in everything and within ourselves, located deep within our heart centres.

Shamans understand the connection to everything, the whole. We have knowledge of our light filaments which spread out above, below, backwards and frontwards, and how these connect us to every living thing in this world and in other dimensions. We know that we are agents of light, working for the Divine as part of a great plan; therefore we are not separate, but conjoined by the vessels of love and light.

Although, it has to be said, it seems the idea of anything Shamanistic is often ridiculed and classed as being pagan, heathen or even a cult! Shamans work on many levels with the unseen worlds. That is how we get help and healing for those who come to see us.

This story illustrates this very well:

When the missionaries came in amongst the indigenous tribes to spread the word of God, they came holding the Bible. A prominent tribesman asked the missionary what it was he was holding, who replied: 'This book is the word of God'. The tribesman took the Bible into his own hands and held it up to his ear... 'I cannot hear anything,' the tribesman said... 'How can I believe in a God that I cannot hear... my God talks to me by way of the rivers, the trees and the mountains'!

Therefore, in answer to the question: 'What do Shamans believe in?' I reply: 'We believe in *all* things': Nature, the Cosmos, and the invisible web that links all of us. We believe in the unseen worlds, the invisible; we believe in the pure power of energy, whether that energy comes from human or from nature. We believe that any rock or stone has a story to tell us. We believe in contact with natural energy beings. We believe that the Earth has a heartbeat and that the stars are our Brothers and Sisters. We see through the illusion of the materialistic world and man's fervent need for power and greed.

I would like to introduce the next Chapter, as it portrays how we as humans absorb ourselves in trying to satisfy an inherent emptiness, which comes from our disconnection to the web of life. Religion has indoctrinated us into believing that we have become separate from God, thrown out of paradise because we didn't toe the line. I want to illustrate how we attempt to fill this sometimes unknowing feeling of our fractures.

For many of us the way we behave, or consume the negative experiences of life, is played out in a fervent need to compensate for our sadness and lack. In doing so many voids are created in our lives. Some of these may come as a surprise and some you may be in denial about; but it is time for us to look at what feeds the dark emptiness in the dark recesses of our stomachs.

Once we are aware of them, maybe then we can start to mend them and return ourselves to harmony and balance. This is only possible if we choose to be aware and choose to change something. This is the first stage on our path of assuming 'right relationship'.

Chapter 3

A Journey into the Emptiness of the Void

If we are to understand how we have become disconnected, we must first recognise what it is to nurture an inner barrenness.

We in the Western world think that we are all doing so well, but if we are, why do we constantly reach out, looking for something to make ourselves feel better, happier and more at ease?

The void (or emptiness) is such an important issue to be aware of. Why is that? The void is such an anomaly, a vast unfamiliar territory which we are unable to navigate as we cannot see or feel it.

Many of us have so often experienced a feeling of emptiness in the pit of our stomach. Our mind informs us that it is not a physical thing, so it can't be important, even though we know it exists because it contains some well known emotions; *fear, nervousness, anger, guilt, shame and anxiety*. It is an unknown invisible black space; a bit like a worm hole that exists deep in the universe. Although this black hole is situated deep within our own personal universe (the physical body) it is just like the holes out in deepest space. Are we too fearful to go into them… just in case we are never seen again?

Let's walk further into the Abyss

This is the emptiness that we superficially try to satisfy or fill. It is a space that constantly needs nourishment and feeding in order for us to feel warm and fuzzy again. The warmth we require is like a lovely soft blanket that is placed around our shoulders while we sit in front of a log fire, drinking hot chocolate, without a care in the world.

Consciously, we do not know why we constantly need to feed it and therefore employ various ways of doing so. Although they *do* all have one characteristic in common... they are usually *detrimental* in some way or another to our mind and body.

Whether you are a prince or a pauper, filling an invisible hole is a mammoth task. I would say that most of us have, at some time, become a victim of this void, and have indulged in many ways over the years to fill it; all in the vain attempt to achieve that ultimate contentment, which is to feel safe and to experience personal bliss.

Let me share with you how the void was illustrated to me in a dream...

I awoke one night, in the middle of February 2009, from a dream. As I was writing this chapter at the time I knew it was a visionary explanation.

The Dream

I was standing in front of a very deep and densely blackened lake. You could not see beneath the surface, and the water was incredibly uninviting! I remember looking at it for a while, frightened to even go close to it... finally with an incredible sense of fear and human curiosity I summoned up the courage to plunge my hands into the water! As they slowly went beneath the cold, black surface, I felt an eel-like head attached to a long body that had a tail that sank deep down into the darkness and depths of the water; its head was near the surface, mouth wide open.

I had no idea what was going on. Before long people got to hear of this lake and it became a curiosity to many who were compelled to come and see it. I watched how the people, who visited the lake to see the creatures, did so in fear and soon enough made pilgrimages to the lake to feed these eel-like creatures. I watched as they threw food and offerings into the water. Surprisingly I noticed that it appeased the creatures; and in feeding them we all knew we would be safe for a while.

27

Eventually news spread of this phenomenon and the scientists got involved, intrigued by the way the villagers were conducting themselves and paying homage to these creatures. They came and conducted tests on the creatures in the lake. They discovered that they had been there since prehistoric times, and we were treating these creatures, just like ancient cultures of the past had... as Gods. What was really evident is how everyone instinctively knew how to keep these creatures appeased and hidden beneath the depths of the water, very careful not to allow them to show themselves above the surface. Instinctively we all knew that the moment the creatures were allowed out there would be complete mayhem!

The dream emphasised to me how we try to still our own inner emptiness and sadness, appeasing and quashing those feelings of lack to keep them sweet, desperately attempting to hide our disquiet, fearful of opening a proverbial can of worms, fearful of unloading our despondency onto the world. Was the void another aspect of our shadow self that we kept hidden from view?

Now that we are all aware of how the emptiness feels let's look at the methods we employ in our modern society in an attempt to make it all better. Some of them will not come as a surprise, some of them you may actually disagree with, but there may be one that you *do* have an affinity with that may surprise you!

Alcohol

Coming home from work, feeling tired and harassed and reaching for a glass of wine or a refreshing vodka and tonic. Sipping it slowly, you sit down and eventually you start to feel the day drain away. In your mind you replay how angry you felt when 'Bob from accounting wanted you to re-do your expense sheet' when you already had a million other things to do.

As your body relaxes, you now have the energy to talk to your wife/husband, help the kids do their homework, and you feel safe within your own castle walls.

For some one glass isn't enough and you find it takes more and more before you find peace and relax. The glass eventually becomes a bottle and you spend most of your free evenings in a stupor.

On the other hand, you may have spent the evening in the pub, with or without friends, downing one drink after another. It is packaged as being social, but as the amount consumed increases the real intent is to block something out, a temporary distraction from real life. Either way, you eventually have to sleep and inevitably you have to wake up in the morning, get up, and start the day all over again, the same old routine. Nothing changes.

Shopping

Picture this: you have had a busy morning at work, it is your lunch hour, you go out to get something for that night's dinner. Maybe you go to Marks & Spencer to get something easy to cook? On the way through the shop you see a jumper, you like the look of it and you buy it! Nothing wrong there, until you realise that you also need a skirt or trousers to go with it! Maybe even a new pair of shoes too?

The next day comes around and it is lunchtime again. Off you go and you pass a shop that is selling bed linen. You see a beautiful Egyptian cotton duvet and go into the shop. Although it is a little pricey, you still buy it. You then notice that it has matching sheets, pillowcases and a gorgeous throw. So you buy them as well! Before you know it, you have spent £150... and you walk out of the shop feeling as sick as a dog!

The weekend arrives and you go out to get the weekly groceries. While walking around the superstore you come to the new electrical appliance section. Here you see a lovely modern toaster or kettle; even though there is absolutely nothing wrong with the devices you already have, you buy them and add them to your grocery basket. After all, it all goes on the food budget.

Shopping is like a covert drug, as on the surface it is a normal enough pass-time... after all, who doesn't love going out at the weekend for a spot of retail therapy? The question is this: how much stuff do we actually need? How many times can we use materialistic acquirement to help us feel better or whole again?

Truthfully, that is *not* what I am illustrating here. Shopping can become a distraction just like any other emptiness filler. You feel unhappy, or someone or something has disappointed you... the niggling hollow cries out to be satisfied... you simply do not know why you keep buying things... as the actual purchase may or may not make you feel better for longer than 30 minutes...

Eating

Oh my! This is another toughie, as we all have to eat to survive. However, this is not about nourishment... this is hardcore comfort eating.

You may be familiar with this scenario: after a busy day, working, running errands, picking up the kids from school, feeding and bathing them and putting them into bed, finally you sit in front of the TV, and you can relax; to reward yourself you polish off a lovely chocolate bar. Mmmm! Or you come home from work; it has been such a stressful day and you head straight for the biscuit or bread bin; need I say more?

Commonly after a seemingly stressful week, to celebrate the weekend, it is very easy to get through an amazing 10,000 calories by consuming the abundance of food that is on offer. No wonder there are many problems involving our digestive systems, diabetes and liver disorders, and obesity.

If we look at how much we comfort eat, we have to be aware that nowadays we live in a society that has an abundance of food products (many of them instant). It is so easy to reach for a food item that will momentarily generate a sense of solace and comfort. For a short while it reminds us of a time when every-thing was okay, a time when we were safe. Unfortunately, the foods that many of us reach for are high calorific, processed and loaded with fats and sugars.

Gambling

This emptiness filler easily leads to addiction ending up a much bigger problem. In the current climate in 2012, more than ever we see an emergence of 'enticements' that are constantly being played out in the media, trying to tempt you into gambling with the promise of easy winnings.

What is disturbing is how more and more of this new advertising is directed at women...

Whether one plays the weekly lottery, or buys scratch cards, or you bet on the horses, we are all trying to win some extra cash to make our lives better. Maybe we do this in order to buy ourselves out of the mundane, or just to have the means to pay off our debts. Or is it because we think money will make everything alright again?

Drugs

The crucial switch off. The ultimate buzz! This furore of chemically enhanced powders and pills that transports us out of the fires of hell and into the wings of heaven... whether we take them socially or because the once social drug-taking has turned into a full-blown addiction... You will find that this void filler comes with a very nasty sting, and it is one that may see you end up in the gutter or even worse, dead, before it has finished with you.

Drug or alcohol abuse leads us down a very treacherous path into an even greater void where the need to change one's reality in order to lessen the pain of life is paramount. The likely outcome will be just like swimming between islands, desperately trying to land. When you do land, the overwhelming urge is to jump straight back off the cliff again... back into oblivion!

The only trouble with void fillers, drugs being at the top of the list, is that the escapism never lasts long. More often than not, reality always hits you between the eyes or in the wallet.

Taking drugs or alcohol is a plea to shut down or escape, these acts are a real cry for help and proof that many people want to shut this current reality out. The world powers, financiers, and politicians have created a reality which many sensitive souls find turbulent and wrong, so the only way out is a choice to shut out all the noise and disharmony, cheating and mismanagement. Sensitive souls do not feel they have a voice or sometimes have the courage to deploy change. Change has to start with the self in the first instance, when we caretake and keep our own houses clear. Then the bigger house, our world, follows.

Sex

Can sex really be seen as a way to fill a void? It can be when it is taken out of the context of procreation and love. Sexual addiction is now quite a common problem. Both men and women find themselves searching for satisfaction and gratification outside the normal realms of relationships. We live in a world where our sense of self-worth and self-esteem are at a low ebb. For some, one of the main ways to gain validation becomes a sexual conquest; a sexual wild hunt.

Sexual pleasure has become one of those great voyages into the unknown, a need to find such gratification that will sustain the human body in a flux of bliss. Cushioned by a need to find a fulfilling relationship packaged as the greatest love story ever told.

Films often portray an array of characters who easily fall deeply in love, offering us a glimpse of real passion and they always seem to enjoy great sex. The plot unfolds on our silver screens amidst storylines that stretch the boundaries of normality, usually played out by characters that possess perfect bodies and gorgeous faces. Many of us have grown up with the ideal that perfect looking individuals, love, and great sex, is the answer to it all, an experience of true nirvana.

With the insurgence of super heroes, vampire 'hottie' fantasies, *normal* young men and women have a seemingly steeper and sometimes insurmountable mountain to climb. We watch with amazement at how these other-worldly creatures leap, shape-shift, using speeds of light in order to save the heroine while still managing to fall in love and enjoy great sex. These films emasculate even the best of us!

Men and women of all ages sign up to the fact that sex, one of the greatest of emptiness fillers, resolves everything! In reality, sexual fantasy and the ultimate orgasm is so often sought out using pornographic material, films and the internet. Fantasy becomes the ultimate search... the Holy Grail!

Sex for some may even become something that is a sham after drinking copious amounts of alcohol and showing their breasts or butt in public.

Women sometimes seem desperate to be in the driving seat, perhaps in an attempt to ditch the frigid and demure labels placed on them from Victorian times, and when the masculine dishonoured the feminine.

Truthfully, what it is we are *really* looking for is someone to validate our worth; boost our esteem in order that we can find our sense of self, but with romantic ideology forged from fantasy and myth. This emptiness may *never* be filled and the search may be a very long one.

Many moons ago, in a time of ritual and ceremony, young men and women were taught the true pleasure that came with the coming together of two people. Sacred sexuality was honoured, revered and the norm. The older women would teach the young women to experience true pleasure in their bodies and women would teach the younger men how to pleasure and respect women. With the onslaught of the masculine need to conquer and to be in power, sacred sexuality was forgotten as were the initiations and teaching of the younger people.

Sex became something of gratification which could be taken and abused at the whim of men's needs and desires.

The religious doctrines taught us that sex was wrong outside of a marriage performed by the church, and the only reason to undergo the act of sexual union was to procreate, because pleasure of the body were frowned upon and pushed underground into secrecy. Men didn't know how to pleasure women, and women didn't know what their sexual needs were. Soon enough men would either forcibly take what they thought was rightfully theirs or go to places where women sold their sexuality. This is the basis for modern men and women's introduction into sexual pleasure. Now it becomes a wild hunt for both sexes to try to regain the pleasures and bliss of sacred sexuality again, part of the journey towards 'right relationship'.

I know I could go on listing other examples of how we fill our inner emptiness, even simple actions, like an obsessive use of the internet, chat rooms and computer games; these can all be seen as ways of switching off from reality, in the search of sating our sadness and disharmony. The real truth behind the search for filling the emptiness lies much deeper, since the void fillers are mere distractions, steering us away from finding our true sense of self. *Not* the self that involves 'I' or 'Me', but the self that has become disconnected from the whole.

Navigating the Void

We now understand the void is a mysterious nothingness that makes you feel empty inside, often indicating that something is missing in your life. It is not like a car that has run out of petrol, or a stomach that has run out of food, as those are simple to replenish.

You may not know *exactly* what it is that you are looking for, but your current lifestyle may provide you with some clues.

This emptiness is not selective; it can be experienced whether you are a wealthy person, an intellectual, or even one who is fighting day by day to keep your head above water. Sometimes, on the surface, your life seems to have everything it needs: a supportive partner, wonderful children, a great job, living in the right place and so on. And yet still you sense that something is missing.

Maybe you are living your life without a partner, or you are involved in a relationship that isn't right for you. You may hate your job or the place you live. Even your children might be giving you problems.

As your life is already full of so many fragmented aspects, you may think that your emptiness can be attributed to your problems. Perhaps you have too many other avenues within your life that need fixing; or you think that 'if only my partner was kind' or 'I wish I had a better job' or 'I wish my kids respected me'... then and only then, would my life become more complete. Of course all of that would certainly help.

Are we disconnected from having a true sense of relationship?

Now, let us look at this emptiness in a spiritual or sacred sense... What if the emptiness is purely down to how we as humans have disconnected ourselves from the Divine or an inherent belief system as I have spoken about in the previous chapter?

Maybe your life is too much out of balance. This doesn't mean a normal work-private life type of balance, but more a dis-harmony, namely a dis-harmony between your three needs, a healthy Mind, Body and Spirit. Many of us can achieve maybe the first two, but the third is often neglected or ignored.

Loss of Faith

Fact... It is not unusual for humans to attain a healthy mind and body, given that there are millions of books, DVDs and television programmes that afford us the information on how to do so. However, there is a tendency for humans to neglect their spirit or sacred pathway.

As we have discovered, we now live in an era in which religions have lost their vice-like grips on their communities, specifically for those of us who live in the West. As said in the previous chapter, maybe the emptiness is connected to being *disconnected* from having 'faith'. The basis of this is having faith in yourself, others, the Earth and the Cosmos. Loss of faith leaves us floundering alone, so how do we start to rebuild an authentic relationship?

Chapter 4

An Authentic Right Relationship

What is this word 'Relationship' all about? Surely now, in our evolved states of awareness, we fully identify with all manner of relationships?

Human beings are extremely involved with their own identity, so much so, it is somewhat difficult for us to think of anything more significant and important outside of us...

The word 'authentic' often tends to get used glibly when someone is trying to make an extra special point that something is genuine, the real deal.

Many of us who follow a spiritual path will use this word to indicate that something isn't illusory, it is heart-centred. But what does 'An Authentic Relationship' really mean?

In terms of philosophy, Authenticity is the conscious self being seen as coming to terms with being in the materialistic world, and with encountering external forces, pressures and influences that are very different to the self. Authenticity is the degree in which one is true to one's own personality, and spirit or character, despite these pressures.

Let's take this further and deeper into the degree of loss of faith and one's sacred and spiritual pathway. Inauthenticity is being unable to be true to one's own sacred heart's desires and spiritual needs.

Socrates stated: 'The unexamined life is not worth living'... therefore, if we live a life in which we are not true to our spiritual needs and we live a life where we ignore responsibility for ourselves, our actions and needs, perhaps that is when we are left out in the cold, floundering like a landed fish. In psychology, a common definition of 'Authenticity' refers to the attempt to live one's life according to the needs of one's inner being, rather than the demands of society or one's early conditioning. This could well point us in the direction of our first encounters with a dogmatic religion, or indeed our parents' and grandparents' belief systems.

So now we know that Authenticity means that we should live a life true to our physical and spiritual needs. But let's expand on this by saying that when we have an absence of a faith in anything, then are we truly living an inauthentic life. In fact, are we truly experiencing an inauthentic relationship to ourselves, others, the Earth and the Cosmos?

The Authentic Self

If the statistics are correct, 18% of people do not believe in any sort of spirituality, God or life force. I would hazard a guess that this figure is possibly much higher. Therefore, we can assume that the amount of disconnection to anything spiritual is a factor when we discuss how humans fill the void that would have been filled by awakening to their spiritual evolution. This, in turn, raises the question, why have people turned their backs on either having faith or a spiritual path? Possibly one reason for this is to do with going through a range of bad life experiences.

Andrew Cohen (a spiritual teacher) states: 'The self beyond ego is said to represent humanity at its most wholesome, creative and compassionate; motivated by an evolutionary impulse that is 'one with the big bang itself'.'

According to Cohen when human beings choose to live as the Authentic Self they can realise their inseparability from the universe and therefore discover a purpose for living that transcends egoism; namely the unique human capacity to participate in the evolution of consciousness itself. (Consciousness is a term used to refer to a variety of aspects between the mind and the world it interacts with; it is an innate ability to experience feelings, awareness and a sense of self).

To be able to have an authentic relationship with yourself, you must first heal the wounds and bad experiences that forced you to disconnect from your wholesome and compassionate life. If you find yourself at a place where this is what you want to do, especially to drop the role of the wounded victim, then it is time to remove all of the toxic sludge that has replaced your light energy with a heaviness and a void that you have been trying to satisfy. When we are disconnected from our authenticity, we also disconnect from being in proper relationship with others and the Earth. (See the chapter on Masculinity & Femininity to further understand relationships with others).

If you recognise the wounded victim archetype, then do not feel despondent, there is something you can do to start the process of your own personal healing journey. Shamans take many routes and avenues when they are looking for a release from their wounds and issues. This may be in the form of a 'read-a-thon', where we look to find an answer to the emptiness; or we ask ourselves; surely there *must* be more to life than this? Or we may undertake an alternative healing journey. Whatever route we take, we understand that it is essential to *take responsibility for our route to wholeness*.

With this in mind, I would like to suggest the following exercise as a way of starting the ball rolling...

Exercise:
How to Heal our Inner Barren Landscape

Before you start, I suggest you read over the steps in order to get a good idea of the processes. Remember to be patient with yourself; do not rush it and do not expect magic. You must put in the work as the processes suggest.

Before you carry on, it is important to always make your intention clear, especially when you are about to undertake any healing journey. Take a moment and ask yourself to commit to taking a step towards wholeness. Let spirit know that your intention is clear. When you ask spirit for help, spirit *always* answers you.

When you are ready, sign a contract for yourself...

CONTRACT

I (your name)................................... Agree to take whatever time I need to in order to find myself once more. I give myself permission to find personal space in order to take on this challenge.

I (your name)............................... undertake the challenge to heal whatever wounds that have been buried deep within my psyche.

I (your name)..........................agree that the time is right to change my life.

SIGNED:

..

Follow the steps below, slowly and mindfully.

Step One: Recognition

We firstly need to recognise the source of your unease; what was the wound or bad experience which started you on a path of unhappiness?

To do this you have to map your life backwards to track the source, the origination of when circumstances urged you to employ a negative behavioural pattern; what kick-started your disconnection from your true essence; what was it that propelled you to void-fill?

Sit quietly and work through these questions. Write the answers in a journal, maybe entitle the journal... I (*your name*) , would like to heal myself.

This is a voyage of discovery; it may be difficult to go back to the event which harmed you. If you find it upsetting or too emotional, before you start, light a candle and say to yourself... 'I am safe and loved by the Divine, the truth cannot harm me'... If it's still too painful, take it slowly, a little at a time. Remember to take some deep breaths and centre yourself before you start.

What was the event that wounded or hurt you?

When were you last really content and happy? (Put an age to that).

What changed?

What happened?

Who changed it?

When were you last in control of your life? (Put an age to that).

Who or what stripped you of control?

What part did you play in the event?

Did you instigate the harm?

When can you remember starting to use something to fill a void?

What do you use to comfort yourself with?

When you have answered all these questions, stand in front of a mirror and state the questions and answers out loud to yourself.

Remember the truth cannot hurt you.

(Please Note: If the discovery is too painful then please do talk to a trusted friend, or family member, or even a GP).

Step Two: Acceptance

Now that you have recognised and stated out loud the origin of your wound, there isn't any mystery attached to it anymore. Maybe you had kept the secret deep within your psyche, or perhaps you had buried it deeply away, and it had almost been a secret you have been keeping even from yourself.

Sometimes the secrets we bury deep within are too painful to allow out. By doing this they niggle away at our emotional body, or create emotional illnesses such as anger, anxiety, depression or even a disorder. That is why it is so important to recognise these dark events and shed light on them, so there isn't any mystery attached to the way you behave.

Now step two comes into play, as we fully accept why or who we have become as a result of being a victim of what happened. Perhaps you had an even greater part to play in what happened; were you the perpetrator? This is the time to go back to the mirror and take a look at how the event took its toll on our psyche, face or expressions.

Are you ready to forgive yourself, or the person or event which has haunted you all these years? Remember, whether you were or were not responsible for the wound, the way you have dealt with it over the years is down to you. That is what I mean by acceptance; taking ownership and accepting responsibility for becoming responsible!

The event happened… fact! How we choose to deal with it is down to us.

Step Three: Stop, Breathe, Relax

Stop punishing yourself… Right now! It's time to rest and revive yourself. Do not do anymore soul-searching for the next week. Now is *not* the time to make huge changes. I suggest some TLC. Eat well, enjoy the fresh air, maybe book a massage, buy a good book; just take each day and do something that pleases you.

It is time to let steps one and two sink in. Remember that there isn't anything to hide away from, or punish yourself for. Maybe use a mantra (a positive statement); write one down, and stick it to the fridge, cupboard door, dressing table, wardrobe, bathroom mirror, car steering wheel, anywhere that you will see it daily.

You can use this one if it sits right with you, 'ALL THAT I KNOW ABOUT MYSELF AND MY PAIN CAN NO LONGER

HURT ME'.

There is nothing better than unleashing a secret or darkly repressed wounding as it lessens its hold on you; your affinity to it is lessened.

So for the next week, eat, rest, read, walk and nurture yourself. Take this time to start the healing process.

Step Four: Heal the Wound

There are several ways to do this and I want to discuss some of the home-healing or self-healing methods.

Firstly, if you haven't done so already *and* you feel able to, confide in someone you trust; a friend or family member. Talk about the wound or event that got you to where you are now.

If you can let it out into the open, Spirit (or the Divine) hears you and knows that you are willing to change your life. By refusing to keep the information to yourself; it is not a secret anymore. It will become *just* an event or wounding.

Write a letter

If the wound or event involves another person, write a letter to them. Be succinct in your feelings and explain how it affected you; how it left you. This is a letter that will never be sent. This is a letter that will be released to Spirit and dealt with on the energetic level.

Before you sign the letter, and if you are willing to do so, add a last paragraph.

This is the way to cease the wound's ability to have an affinity with you. It is always that affinity that burrows deep into our psyche and energy body and informs us in a negative way... urging us to damage ourselves in some way or another. The affinity becomes emphatic in its make-up.

For example: If you had your leg amputated... obviously at the time you would be awfully miserable and mourn the loss of your leg...

eventually when time has passed you realise that you could still live a decent enough life; you had become used to living without your leg; then one day, you see another person who has just lost their leg... they were terribly upset about it... It is THEN that the affinity comes into play. Why? It's because it is human nature to delve back to the time when you first lost your leg. All of the same feelings and misery that surrounded that event will come flooding back to you. For a while you are lost in those feelings that you had long forgotten about... and suddenly your psyche and energy body are once again informed from the place of your initial wounding, the initial loss. And for however long it takes, you will feel damaged again by that loss.

Write the last paragraph as one of forgiveness. Now, forgiveness used in this context is not one of: 'I forgive you' because I am letting you off the hook! No, the forgiveness here is one where you release and cut the ties once and for all with the event or wound. Once this has been done it can no longer harm you. So write something along the lines of (use what wordings are appropriate): 'I forgive you/myself (or what happened) for what it did to me/what I did to another person'; 'I know that at the time you/I were in a negative place where you/I needed to hurt somebody'; 'I understand what a place that can be, so I need you to know that I am releasing the wounds connected to the event and therefore I wish you (or I wish to live) a peaceful life.'

That is all you need to say.

Step Five: Burn the Letter

(Remember: *Whenever you light a fire inside, make sure that you use either a fireplace, or a candle placed in a fire-proof bowl. If you choose to go outside, then make sure that you only light the fire in a safe environment, away from dried grass, hay or trees*).

Now it is time to release the past, to give it away to spirit. This will allow you to release the affinity from your psyche and energy body. You have given enough penance to the event or wound over the years. It is time to go outside to a quiet spot. Ask Spirit or the Divine to take away all the pain and suffering, release the affinity you may have to the words in this letter; turning all that heavy toxic energy into light, abundant, positive energy. Get ready to set light to it. Ensure all of the paper and every word is consumed in the flames. As you watch it burn, feel how wonderful the feeling of release is. Just as the last piece of paper turns to smoke, use your hand to draw the smoke into your belly; then your heart and then your head. This in turn replaces the heavy toxic energy into light flowing energy.

For the remaining ash that is left dig a small hole in the soil and bury it.

Step Six: Rest, Breathe, Relax

Rest again for the next week, allowing yourself time to recuperate from all of the healing and releasing. It will allow you to re-access yourself to see where you are now.

Do you feel now that you have recognised the wounding or event?

Have you accepted the details of the wound or event?

Have you released your affinity to the wound or event?

Do you feel lighter?

Do you feel stronger?

Has the hold of the negativity shifted?

Do you feel more peaceful and lighter?

Are your thoughts more positive?

If you answer mainly *yes* to these then:

For the next week, eat, rest, read, walk and nurture yourself. Take this time to continue the healing process. Just be mindful to note how you are feeling.

If you answer *no* to most of the above or you still feel negativity towards the wound or event (or if you still feel confused) then write down your feelings. As soon as the words come they will reaffirm the acknowledgement.

It is okay to still feel angry or to experience frustration at this juncture. Writing down exactly how you feel is both cathartic and healing. Read the words out aloud and set fire to them. If you still experience problems recognising or accepting the event or wound and you are experiencing anger, despair or frustration, try this:

Sit Quietly

Sit quietly in a place where you will not be disturbed. Have a pen and paper ready. Make sure that the place is where you can sit in silence (turn off phones, radios and TVs). Make sure that you are comfortable and not distracted with any type of aches or pains. Close your eyes. Take some deep breaths in for the count of seven; hold the breath for a count of seven; and release the breath for a count of seven. Repeat this process seven times. Keeping your eyes closed, allow your mind to examine what it is that is making you feel angry or frustrated. Focus all your energy on that emotion. When you have it in your sights, ask these questions:

Why am I frustrated?
What is making me angry?
Where does this feeling come from?

What happens during the process is this: as you track for the wound within the silence you disassociate yourself from the mind's influence so it can't offer up the same old story or information. Shamans call this our well-rehearsed script; you know the one, as it is the story you tell yourself or others about the effects of your wounding over and over again; a script we get to know well. It becomes part of our own personal myth.

Instead, what is required is this: the memory-impulses in our bodies inform us from a place of truth as we travel the path towards enlight-

enment. As the emotion travels around our body, it is then the real facts emerge, stronger and more succinct. Be patient, it may take 30 seconds to reveal the answer, or it may even be longer. The point here is to accept and trust in the silence and wait! When you have the answer, write it down; write the whole event down... read it out aloud... then burn it.

Repeat the beginning of this step (six) again, asking yourself the questions and see if you can answer yes to most of them now.

Step Seven: Decision

Now you will have arrived at a point where one of two things will happen, you will either feel more peaceful and settled now that you have ousted the demon, or you will still feel that you have something more to tackle. You may feel at a loss as you don't know what to do next. If the latter is still true then please get some professional help! I suggest more 'alternative' help at this stage. Either see a Shamanic practitioner (*I recommend that they have been trained by the Four Winds, as you will get a professional and thorough healing*), or see an Acupuncturist who can help release the stress and anxiety through the body's meridians (as well as dealing with other issues). Alternatively, see a Homoeopathist or a Qualified Medical Herbalist who will help you at the cellular level, as well as move you forward and help provide you with much more clarity. If you do not fancy going down this route, consider psychotherapy or counselling.

Step Eight: Perception

It's time to look at negative behavioural patterns; these are formulated out of the way you perceive yourself, your life or other people.

Perception belongs in the realms of the ego; it is created from an idea, never a fact. We battle and mull these ideas around in our heads when we are trying to rationalise something that doesn't serve us, or something that doesn't fit into our own rationale. We believe that these ideas belong solely to us. After all, everything that pops into our heads must be right, surely?

How can it be right?

What is it that allows us to be the authority on everything?

Oh, I know, our ego says it... well that's okay then. But it is not okay, is it?

Because the way we perceive something may or may not be the right way.

Who determines which is the right or wrong way after all? Humans? If it is humans then again it is only the opinion of the one who perceives it and surely that is a subjective opinion after all. Only the right way can be validated when it comes from the absolute truth or fact.

The only way to prove or disprove this fact is to find out the truth. Bringing truth to a situation allows us to step out of the grip of ego, and into the realm of truthful knowledge. We do this by determining the truth of any given situation, ensuring that our perception has been informed from a place of knowledge. How we choose to deal with that knowledge is a learning curve that ensures we grow. It is all about being impeccable.

Take your journal and sit quietly and mull over the relationships you have...

Are you judgemental towards people?

Do you gossip or join in gossiping about others?

Are you racist, ageist or even sexist?

Are you opinionated about other people's lives?

Spend about 15 minutes examining the way you perceive other people.

Step Nine: Change

Signing up to change a behavioural pattern takes a little more effort because it has probably become a mindset or a routine. Often we find we do or say things without thinking; our thoughts are automatic rather than systematic. The changes we are required to make here have to be mindful; not calculated, but careful.

Changing a pattern or damning behavioural trait takes patience, as much as you would need if you were to train a new puppy. If you are the type of person who says or does things without thinking about another's feelings or respecting someone's space, then you will need to change that and become *more* aware of another's feelings or space.

For example: Foisting your opinions on others; telling others what to do; demanding too much from another; barging in and invading another person's space without an invite. These are all personal invitations to check yourself.

Try to start this process easily by eliminating the phrases *'shouldn't you...'*, *'don't you think you should...'* or *'do this, will you?'* from your vocabulary. Try to eliminate the ability to gossip or judge. Check your aggression or body language. Remember, if we change our behaviour to that which serves us better, then we can become a shining example to others.

While you undertake the magic of any energy healing, please take the time to allow it to gently resonate with your mind, body and spirit.

Read on, as the next chapters take you on a further experiential journey, looking at relationships and also examining some of the pitfalls many of us find ourselves falling into.

Chapter 5

Right Relationship with Others

Okay, now we know what an authentic right relationship is. Let us see how our adaptation of our own personal relationships affects us. Where do our emotional wounds come from? How does our perception of our relationships become so disillusioned in reality?

This subject is hard to divulge, let alone write down in an intelligible form.

This is purely down to relationships being such a contentious subject matter and the fact that *everyone's* versions and expectations of a relationship are *so* different.

Let me say at this point that I am NOT a relationship guru by any stretch of the imagination.

My views come from the many observations that I have made during my own relationships; with myself, parents, husband, children and from clients who have visited me for healing regarding their relationship problems.

Sadly, but true, around 50% of the clients who visit me have had many problems understanding their relationships with others. Top of the list would be women's relationships with men or men's relationships with women.

They usually come to me with a mixture of the following questions:

'Why can't I get a partner?'
'Why can't I get on with people?'
'Why can't I find someone who will love me?'
'Why can't I find a partner who will understand me?'
'Why am I alone?'

Now, as a Shamanic practitioner, I will facilitate and remove any affinity to a relationship wounding that may have affected them. I do this by using a range of Shamanic practices that I have been taught. But *still* they expect me to conjure true love for them!

Again, I must stress that I am *not* a trained relationship psychologist...

I wonder, however, why there are so many different perspectives and so much time spent on the subject of relationships with others. Why is it in this modern age that some men and women have such a hard job nurturing a relationship with the opposite or same sex?

Is it down to the fact that each one of us expects too much?

Is it because we already have such a fragile relationship with ourselves and the world around us?

Do we actually know what a relationship is?

Are we capable of giving that much of ourselves?

Some say that in romantic love we 'expect everything and get nothing'... while in an arranged match we 'expect nothing and get everything'! Others say that romantic love is a 'cruel trick of nature to propagate the human race' and has nothing to do with marriage and should be tried out many times to get it out of one's system!

(The Secret Places of the Burren) John M Feehan

Hitting a Brick Wall

Many of us 'hit a brick wall' at some point in our lives. This 'wall' often occurs during our 40s; a significant time in our lives, so often written and talked about... and usually labelled the mid-life crisis.

From my point of view, I would say that having a mid-life crisis is more likely down to either questioning something or a reluctance to enter into another stage of our lives. Maybe it is just a cliché intended to encourage us to look more closely at our own lives?

If you are in a partnership with someone of a similar age to you, then it is likely that both of you will hit this 'brick wall' at a similar time. So where are our role models when we need help with this subject? Do we go to our parents, siblings, friends or a counsellor?

The fact is this: the people we usually turn to for help are more than likely to have had comparable experiences regarding relationships to ours. If you are in any doubt, just look at the divorce statistics, instances of separation, or the number of one-parent families that make up our society. The relationships we have with our partner, spouse, mother, father, work colleague, neighbour, friends, siblings, are surely where most of the problems begin in the first place.

Again, who do we learn from?

Of course, we may be lucky enough to have parents who are wonderful role models. You could spend time asking them but you may find that their own method for coping with relationships is more likely down to luck or sticking with it rather than a tried and tested relationship formula.

My Own Experience With Relationships

In my own life, I can remember the first time I questioned my relationship with my husband. He was in his early 40s and I was four years younger. It was the first time we had experienced a 'problem'.

Even as a child growing up I never thought about relationships, whether they were with my mother, father, grandparents, friends or boyfriends. After all, my mother and father seemed to have a solid relationship; my grandmother must have experienced true love as she lived her life nursing a broken heart following the death of her husband. As far as I knew, I was surrounded by people who knew love... or was I? As I learnt in later life, often the knowledge of love is based around one's own idealistic perception.

My mother and father seemed to get on well. They did not argue much, other than the odd bicker here and there. My father was very laid back about everything; my mother had a quick temper always telling me that her bark was worse than her bite. Quite simply, I thought that everything was just great with them. The shock for me came long after dad died. Mum told me that she had lived most of her married life lonely in her relationship with my father. Now, as I am older, I realise that maybe it wasn't all that it seemed... maybe our family rapport was purely superficial as we hardly ever delved beneath that surface, or wanted to go any deeper into knowing what others were really thinking, feeling or experiencing.

Not that I am decrying my childhood; it was wonderful. But the question is, did I have a fulfilling relationship with them all? I guess to answer that I really would have to understand more about the expectations of our relationships from all family members concerned.

Okay, returning to my relationship with my husband... As mentioned, Paul was in his early 40s; we had both enjoyed an extremely good social life, going out with friends and having fun as though we were still in our 20s! Paul and I would go out together on a Friday night. It was a bit like a 'date night'; *our* time to unwind. Our nights out usually involved consuming a fair amount of alcohol. Slowly, but surely, the alcohol did *not* serve us as well as it used to... or should I say that our bodies no longer coped with the toxicity as well as they used to.

Like many other couples we had very busy working lives, children to care for and a house to keep. However, we found that the frustrations of the week did not suit us as a couple. Suddenly, everything became more of a negative than a pleasure. Indeed, it was quite stressful as we were both trying to unwind and reset ourselves to recover from such busy lives.

We found that we began to suffer from the relentless early mornings whilst trying to maintain enough energy for the rest of the day and evening. At the time, Paul was struggling with his own personal wounds relating to events in his early childhood, alongside the never-ending strains of maintaining a busy, high-powered job.

His struggle started to play havoc and eventually manifested in several ways... His self esteem began to suffer and a constant need to please others just got too much (one of those being me). He told me that he did not feel good enough. He felt that the masculine role as main provider for me and the girls, alongside his role of father and husband was slowly being chipped away. His energy was being zapped!

The strong emotions he was experiencing daily were weakening him. Even the responsibility of providing a roof over our heads was becoming more and more stressful. He was getting emotionally weaker and weaker. Despite this, he was and still is, an amazing father to our girls. To this day I have not seen too many fathers that give so much of their time to their children as he does.

However, very soon, events relating to Paul's past were beginning to implode. These mainly consisted of the roles relating to being a son and a brother. More and more, Paul filled his void with alcohol as his way of unwinding. He would use this as an attempt to switch off his ego and the constant mind chatter he was experiencing. As you can guess, this only served to create yet more demons than he had before. His attempt to keep his life normal by relaxing and having a drink after work did not help as the quick pint would sometimes turn into several.

Needless to say, it was during that time that I began to feel vulnerable. The feelings of uneasiness (my emptiness) turned into an obsession with food (my void filler). After all, I came from a fairy tale upbringing, didn't I? And in fairy tales, love never goes wrong, does it?

Paul and I were beginning to drift apart from each other. I was feeling vulnerable and Paul became distant. He was starting to shut off from me and had stopped confiding in me as much as he used too. He could not cope with what was going on inside his head. He seemed to be on the back foot and felt that he had to constantly apologise to us. I did not know if he still loved me. I did not know whether he would eventually hurt or even kill himself. When he drank there was an incredible tension between us and he was becoming harder to please. Any type of communication between us became fractious, and of course, our sexual relationship was declining, a time bomb waiting to go off.

During that period in our lives I went into survival mode. I 'donned a mask' by pretending that everything was just fine, especially in front of our parents, friends and, of course, our daughters, even though I knew that they were not blind or deaf.

Obviously his drinking was a cry for help. Even though he is an extremely intelligent man, he had no idea of what, if any, help was available to him.

We knew it was *not* the alcohol that had caused the problem. It was what Paul and *his issues* had become with alcohol inside him. He was adding alcohol to all of his daily stresses, anxieties, woundings and family history; a mixture that became a very toxic cocktail.

Finally and thankfully, the unthinkable happened! (to this day I believe 'a higher being' finally intervened). On October 1st 2001, Paul decided to stop drinking and he has not had a drink since. Paul knew that the lethal mixture of alcohol and emotions would only have one outcome. Obviously, from that point onwards, life changed dramatically for all of us. Paul had somehow managed to free himself from his 'void filler'; free from the toxicity of alcohol.

I remain forever grateful to him, and so thankful that our love did not diminish as a result... in fact it just got stronger. We knew that we were heading towards another chapter in our lives...

My Relationship With My Own Parents

As painful and honest as it is, I would like to examine the relationship that I have with my own father and mother. I would like to *really* look at the relationship I had with my father. He was, of course, my first experience of a masculine role model.

I remember that we hardly ever discussed anything at length; we never sat down and had a heart-to-heart chat as Paul does with our daughters. Was it down to the fact that he simply did not know how to? After all, *he* had been taught by his own role models; *his* mother and father. My day-to-day experiences with dad usual involved daily repartees such as: 'Good morning', 'How was work?', 'Everything alright?' or 'Good night, love'.

I guess I was as guilty as he was, as I never sparked up a conversation with him. I had inherited his quietness. We did laugh a lot together as he had a wicked sense of humour, which usually came out when he was in company or at the pub. Yes, dad was a 'man's man'.

For many years he enjoyed going to the pub, playing skittles, darts and bowls. That was his escape until he became diabetic. I have since found out that none of these outlets provided my mother with a significant relationship with her husband. In fact, he often left her feeling quite lonely and isolated. They never socialised together at the pub. It was not mum's idea of a good night out.

If I am truthful, I feel quite cheated by not having a close relationship with him. He died in 1992. Sadly, I do not know, and will never find out, what he would have thought about me and how his grandchildren have turned out today. I do know that I miss him a lot. As I am writing this I feel saddened that this is probably the time in my life that I would have developed a close relationship with him. And the sad fact is that he is not here to do so.

Mother-Daughter Relationship

While I was growing up, my relationship with my mother was entirely different. We chatted and had discussions about most things. She was really interested in my life and offered me enormous emotional support.

I understand the feminine role quite well, especially having watched two generations of females in the house (my mother and grandmother). I saw the changes that they had experienced throughout their lives. Mum provided much of what I wanted; more importantly, she provided everything she could...

My current relationship with mum is pretty much the same and lately, during 2012, in some ways, there have been some significant changes. I can only presume these changes are more than likely to be down to me rather than mum as she always remains very constant.

It was inevitable that a change came when Paul and I moved back into mum's home for a while, mainly to regroup and assess the next stage of our lives.

Once again, generational history was repeating itself. Many years ago, when my grandfather died, my mum had *also* moved back in with her mother.

The change that occurred was more to do with my role as an adult daughter and one where I was trying to establish space as a home-maker in a house that already had a head of house; very difficult, to say the least.

The other problem, and one I did not contemplate, was mum's new partner. Initially we were thrilled that she had found a partner to keep her company. What we did not calculate was how the dynamics with him would be critically difficult when we all moved back home. This, of course, forced a wedge between mum and me. As I reflect now about this relationship dynamic I find that the difficulty we experience has more to do with a generational gap and old belief system. This is the 'eggshell path' that is very difficult to tread! As much as we try to find the middle ground, it is still proving very tricky; we are *very* different people.

Harmony Within Relationships

Okay, enough about me! Let me get back to discussing relationships in general.

How do we function and find meaning within our relationships?

Firstly, we need to go back to the relationship that we have with *ourselves*.

Do we respect ourselves?

Do we like ourselves?

Can we be alone with ourselves?

Can we face our inner shadows and accept them?

Do we cherish the body we have been given?

Do we liberally eat fruits and vegetables that provide us with the necessary vitamins and minerals that are required to enable our body to function correctly?

Do we take the right amount of exercise and fresh air?

I am going to leave this section with you to muddle over. After all you are reading about someone who has abused her body with food for the past 20 years in order to try to make herself feel better and cope with stress!

How do we fulfil our needs when it comes to creativity and passion for life?

Are our needs met?

Our Relationship with the Planet

What about your relationship with our Earth?

How do we treat this wonderful planet we live on, the Earth that sustains us, that provides us with all that we need; food, fresh air, freedom?

How do we pay her back?

I know that I have mentioned this before, but again, as with your own body, this planet *must* be nurtured and maintained to enable it to sustain us now and for our children's children in the future.

We must *not* allow it to continue to fall into decay; constantly allowing humans to rape its soils and becoming the *takers* without ever replacing the things that have been taken. This *is* and *should* be the personal responsibility of *all of us!*

Understanding ourselves and the planet we live on are two great places to begin learning about our relationships.

If we have a fear of living and feel that we cannot even love ourselves or the planet, how can we even begin to have relationships with others? As soon as you can say that you respect, honour and love your own body *and* the Mother Earth, *then* and *only then* are you beginning to understand the process of experiencing a healthy authentic right relationship.

Chapter 6

The Archetypical Roles of the Masculine & Feminine

Expectation is a word that can destroy even the best of us, let alone our relationships. Each and every one of us will at some juncture have an expectation of how we view the opposite sex, whether by reasoning or by experience. Is the interpretation behind each sex's representative role purely down to our nature or is it nurtured?

It's Story time... Once Upon a Time there was a Prince

The archetypal masculine role is that of the Adventurer!

When a young Prince is born, he is cosseted by the Queen (his Mother); often seen as a younger version of his King (his Father). He is taught very early on that he should only concern himself in male pursuits. His father is keen on this 'just in case he becomes sick or gay' (again said tongue in cheek)!

He is given masculine toys, swords, cars, footballs and replica weapons. He is taught to play fight and wrestle. At a young age he is also directed towards sporting pursuits and competitive games; football, martial arts and computer games, etc. The overall lesson being that the young Prince learns how to conquer adversity and ultimately win...

His wonderful, adoring Queen teaches him all of the necessary social requirements. He is taught how to treat girls well as they are precious creatures and require respect (hopefully). He is taught to be polite, be clean and to have a measured emotional psyche.

After being educated by the King's Consul and Sages, he learns how to forge himself a great career. This will enable him to make his own way in life and make something of himself.

Now, throughout all of these teachings and within the Prince's own head space and psyche, he is creating his own myth, rather than every-thing the Elders are teaching him. He sees himself forging a pathway to become a warrior, riding a horse and slaying dragons! Even though he has trouble leaving the embrace of his loving Mama (with her gift of a 'warm smothering mantle'), and with the knowing look of his Father, he sets off on his quest. On his journey he meets many other Warriors, Knights and Kings. He soon learns from them many ways of combat and how to conquer; alongside other manly traits such as celebration and pleasures of the flesh!

He spends several moons in combat and winning battles. Very soon after enjoying these pleasures, he starts to notice the opposite sex in a more lusting type of way! He soon finds that he is pursuing a 'comely wench' whom he wishes to make his Princess. He has fallen madly in love with her and wants to take her for his wife.

He soon asks her father (her King) for her hand in marriage. Now, her King is slightly more suspicious of this young warrior! He wants to be assured of the safety of his Princess and to be convinced that this young warrior Prince will provide her with all that she needs.

Eventually the King gives his consent. A wonderfully expensive wedding takes place; the warrior Prince finds his own castle; and he whisks her off to raise a family.

Days go by... he is out slaying dragons and fighting battles and his true love (his young Queen) will be keeping house and cooking his meals.

Finally, as the years go by and the warrior Prince begins to tire of battle, the time comes when he begins to question the path he has forged for himself. He believes that his manhood is slowly creeping away and is not being satisfied! As a consequence, he needs validation, and he feels the need to find and be with other wenches. He does this in order to prove his masculinity, feel worthy again and to make him feel like the young, handsome Prince that he once was!

Sure enough, the wenches and new horses still do not fill his void! As he slowly ages, he finds himself turning to an elder male for counsel, perhaps his father, the King or maybe even an Uncle. Could they help him understand the journey that a young Prince takes in order to become an Elder or a wise King? The words spoken by the Elder male are steeped in wisdom and history. Finally a wonderful peace comes over the 'Man'.

The Prince elects to accept his rites of passage into his sage-hood and he too becomes an Elder. His life slows down to a much quieter pace; he no longer aches for the noise and thrill of battle or the sound of steel upon steel. Instead he becomes content to spend time at home in his castle and to spend his autumn days with his wife. They find quieter pursuits and only very occasionally will he discuss his memories of youthful times in the pursuit of battle and the prizes that he had won.

Such is the myth of the Male!

(Fairytale loosely based on the book *HE* by Robert A Johnson).

The Feminine Fairytale… The Princess

The feminine pathway is a very different tale!

The Princess grows up as the daughter of her proud and adoring King and Queen. She is lavished with attention and presents, freely given to amuse her in the walls of her 'ivory castle'. This 'ivory castle' has been built to keep her safe and protected from all manner of harm; anything bad that may affect her would be spoken about in hushed voices by the King and Queen.

She is looked after well and given gifts a-plenty, including perfect baby dolls that never cry, toy kitchens and dollhouses. The young Princess will learn how to become a Queen and mother herself. She will be given beautiful dressing-up clothes, wonderful items that will whisk her away to her fairytale imaginary world. She will have perfectly-shaped Barbie dolls and handsome Kens and she, too, will have many beautiful, magical and wonderful outfits and jewellery to wear.

The Princess is taught to dance and soon becomes the next Darcey Bussell. She is taught how to eat correctly in order to keep her well. She will spend endless hours in the castle grounds, conversing with small deer and baby rabbits. Bluebirds will serenade her and she will have afternoon tea with the fairies.

One day a young handsome Knight rides into her father's Court! She is totally captivated by his manliness. His overwhelming confidence allows her to feel things she had never felt before. She is flushed with love and expectation, and the handsome Knight does his utmost to win the heart of the beautiful Princess.

The King will make sure that the young Knight is sincere and worthy of his beautiful Princess. In order for the Knight to show that his intentions are honourable, he will set several tasks for the young Knight to complete. When he has finally proven himself, he will be allowed to take the Princesses' hand in marriage!

With the blessing of both the King and Queen, and following a wonderfully expensive wedding celebration, he whisks his new bride away to his own lovely new castle.

Their marriage is blissful and she loves to wait on him. She loves it when he dotes on her! She will wait for him while he goes out on his escapades and welcome him home again with loving arms.

On his return he brings her beautiful gifts. Their unbridled nights of passion provide her with babies. he will bring them up as perfect little beings that one day will also become the next young Knights or Princesses.

Many days go by and one day, while she is sitting in front of the mirror, she notices that her youth is diminishing! She is also beginning to notice that her beloved Knight stays away longer than he used to! The occasions when he brought home gifts have long since ceased.

During her many days of loneliness, constantly trying to keep her youth so that she may be adored once more, she finds herself turning to another Knight! This Knight, having won her over, is hell bent on lavishing his attention on her, as long, of course, as she rewards him with 'pleasure'.

Soon, deep within her heart, she knows that this Knight is only after one thing and isn't sincere in his affections! The fear of losing her standing in society forces her to let him go, and once again she finds herself very lonely.

In her sadness, she turns to the Queen who is also failing in her years. After a quiet counsel with the Queen, she is told how to win back the adoration of her King. She is told that it is now the time for both of them to accept their autumn years together.

After a celebration to enable her to step into her Wise-womanhood, her Croneship, she eventually and happily becomes the Wise woman!

Her Knight finally returns and hangs up his spurs! Together they sit in front of the fire, in quiet contemplation, holding hands and reading stories to their own grandchildren.

Such is the myth of the feminine!

(Fairytale loosely based on the book *SHE* by Robert A Johnson).

These analogies are written in the form of a fairytale. They are very much 'tongue in cheek' to help emphasise and illustrate just how archetypal the roles once were and, more importantly, how archetypically *we* expect *our* lives to be, just like a fairy story. Or is it because we have an unrealistic expectation, a mythic perception of love and relationships?

A Dose of Reality

In most cases, the *reality* is oh so different, isn't it? There is little difference and much confusion between the masculine and feminine roles adopted by men and women today; now they are following such similar stories and pathways.

Nowadays, most girls and boys are brought up equally. They can *both* play with dolls and *both* play with guns. There do not seem to be any definitive masculine or feminine careers any more; women go to war and men become nurses. Both sexes actively pursue their careers, both becoming dedicated and ambitious. Both sexes enjoy the feeling of achievement; both sexes avidly socialise; both travel the world.

Women now drink as much as men and sometimes even more. Some women now take more drugs and party even harder than their male counterparts.

There is so much media focus on how women conduct their sexual relationships. Some, just like men, make sure that they avoid being wounded in the heart by making absolutely sure they adopt a 'sleep with them and leave them attitude'. Perhaps this is payback time for the many times over the centuries that women had been neglected in their sexual pleasure...

Back to the Present

Finally, a women's body clock tick, tick, ticks away... They eventually become tired of their masculine pursuits and find it is time to get themselves a life partner, purely for the sake of procreation, of course. When a suitable mate has been sought and found, they spend thousands of pounds on lavish fairytale weddings. They go on exotic and wonderful honeymoons, and of course, there is the need to buy and furnish the perfect show home nests.

After all of that, if lucky, they get pregnant, bearing in mind that the infertility rate is forever going up.

More and more women have problems conceiving. Not such a surprise, as many women are now either constantly stressed or anxious, or are too body focussed on being wafer thin. After many years of trying to forge a name for themselves in the workplace and constant partying it is small wonder that their bodies find it hard to reproduce.

When the baby finally arrives, it is not unusual for the man to stay at home to look after the child; or perhaps both partners head straight back to their careers to bring home the required 'bucks'; much-needed funding for their over-inflated lifestyles. In this instance, the baby may be placed in childcare, another huge cost. Both sexes will be responsible for the cooking, cleaning and (in some cases) looking after the baby.

The Dynamics of the Roles are Confused

We are creatures of a new concept; a divide has been created:

neither sex has a clearly defined function; the roles have merged into one. The only thing separating them is their gender.

Men no longer feel like the 'warrior' or 'hunter gatherer'; this has long since disappeared. There is no longer the need to go out to gather food; we have supermarkets for that. We now see the emergence of the 'warrior' within the feminine. So much so that women sometimes become very disconnected from their softer sides, seemingly unable to connect to their inner 'goddess' or 'inner princess' for fear of showing their vulnerability.

Both men and women are often confused with their roles and dynamics within a partnership. Neither gender seems to have a definite idea of what is actually required of them anymore. This clearly doesn't help the natural harmony between the sexes, or create a natural harmony within relationships.

Where does a man find his sword? Where does a woman connect to her ability to nurture?

I will say this: men will certainly *not* find their sword at a football match; nor will women find what they are looking for in a boardroom. Maybe it fulfils certain fantasies about power and domination, but that's all. Perhaps, instead, we should concentrate on regaining a healthy balance and respect for both the masculine and feminine genders.

Women do *not* need to prove themselves to men and vice versa for men. What we are forgetting here is the ability to *support* each other in partnership. History has shown us many examples where men have earned the right to hold their swords aloft (metaphorically speaking); and women have earned the right to a voice that should be heard. There is, however, a much more serious problem and that is the ever-growing problem concerning relationship.

Men and women have quite simply forgotten how to relate to each other. Is that down to the confusion and expectation in each other's roles; or because women have emasculated the men; or are men still striving to keep hold of their warrior roles by trying to dominate their mates, even in the 21st Century?

Either way, it eventually comes back down to how we *treat* each other; how we treat ourselves and the world around us. The clue lies in our inability to take responsibility for our own actions and our own words.

Chapter 7

It's all about Communication, Harmony & Perception

Unfortunately, people in the evolved Western world seem to have learnt how to NOT effectively communicate with each other. We may be under some sort of illusion to the contrary, but in truth we have adapted an alternative behaviour of assertiveness, violence and abrasiveness towards each other. Is this perhaps due to the fact that we are constantly on the defensive, or somehow we feel threatened? Or is it because we are too self-involved, confused or simply cannot be bothered?

No small wonder that during these confused times, the masculine and feminine end up so stressed out with each other. It doesn't necessarily mean that we are upset. It is far more likely to be down to the daily grind that has become so monotonous. Each partner is drowning by striving too hard to create something that is unsustainable. Our Western lives have become too hard to maintain.

Today, more so than ever, both partners are working *too hard!* Money *never* seems to stretch far enough and our expectations for our lives are just too high. Even the chores that we create for ourselves are seemingly endless; there is *never* enough downtime because we have become creatures of 'busy-ness'.

It has become so important that we *must* find the time to catch our breath; to unwind, reconnect with that which is missing, reconnect with nature and find ourselves again.

If we do not do this, our souls will feel suffocated; we will not be able to see any light at the end of the tunnel. And then guess what? When humans feel trapped, with no option of escape, *that* is when we are backed into a corner and start to bare our teeth;

and unfortunately, it is usually at the people we care about the most.

We resort to showing emotions that are fed by anger, fear and frustration; turning on those closest to us. We look to blame someone else, as our frustration and anger are too much for us to shoulder alone. We start to dig ourselves into deep holes, slowly putting a strain on our relationships.

We become blameful, picky, withdrawn and unreasonable, especially if we do not feel that we are being listened to or understood. We recoil and pull up a survival shield around us, deploying a well known control drama or even worse, something more damaging. Truthfully, all we want to achieve is to get a little attention.

These attention exploits may even result in us having an affair or something even more self-abusive like losing ourselves in alcohol, drugs, shopping or gambling. Very often the undesired results become like a battle; a raged war and a one-upmanship game with our partner as we harbour thoughts like: 'I'll show him', or 'sod her, I'm off to have some fun'. We place so much energy in the pursuits of battle rather than trying to sort out the problem.

Have we Forgotten How to Talk to Each Other?

Has it really gone so far that we cannot even communicate anymore? Do we have so little respect left for our partner that we would rather just bottle it all up, go out and find another mate, rather than taking the time to mend the relationship? Have relationships become so dispensable?

Why is it that so many couples cannot find the time to sit down with their partner and discuss ways around the problem, make some changes, work out ways to do things differently?

In some cases, I do realise that this is not possible as one of the partners is completely unwilling to make any changes. Perhaps they are so tied up within the 'stress-mess' that they cannot see any way to bring light into the situation. The result of conflict is that we drown in the heaviness of battle, unable to see the possibility of resolution, focussed too much on our own hurt, 'you did this' or 'you said that'. That is what we seem to be more occupied with.

Time to Re-introduce Hucha and Sami – 'A Conflict of Energies'

If you recall, I explained that Shamans believe in two types of energy: Light (Sami) and Heavy (Hucha). Like most polarities (Heavy and Light being one), they are at opposite ends of the scale. They are a conflict of energies.

A conflict of energies is completely relative when we discuss relationships.

To identify how humans interrelate with each other and to illustrate how there are absences of interaction, consider this: most of us *hold onto* Hucha (toxic and heavy energy) and *use it as a weapon* instead of *letting go of its heaviness* and substituting it with a *much lighter energy*.

For example if we have been wounded in the past, whether a wound of the heart or a wound relating to abuse, we inform ourselves from the place of that original wounding. As a consequence, we march forward as a wounded soul or victim, expecting everyone else to *see that* and understand just why we act the way we do.

In some relationships we find a mixture of Light (Sami) and Heavy (Hucha) energy *fighting* for supremacy. It is just like a tug of war, being fed from the frustrations that we hang onto within ourselves.

Let me share an old story…

There is a legend of a conversation between an old Cherokee Indian and his grandson. The message is great but the storytelling is even better. One evening, an old Cherokee Indian told his grandson about a battle that goes on inside people. He said: 'My son, there is a battle going on between two wolves inside us all. One is Evil - It is anger, envy, jealousy, greed, and arrogance. The other is good - It is peace, love, hope, humility, compassion and faith.' The grandson thought about this for a while and then asked his grandfather: 'Which wolf wins?' To which the old Cherokee simply replied, 'The one you feed the most.'

I believe that we *all* have the tendency to feed *both* wolves, but we tend to feed one more than the other. It is usually the wolf that we feed the most that will determine the quality of our lives. If you start to pay attention to this, you will also notice that while you may not be feeding the evil wolf large pieces of beef, you may well be inadvertently throwing it some small scraps!

The Battle Inside

When we are hurt or frustrated we instinctively employ our intellect or ego to find a solution. Inside our heads we analyse it over and over, trying to figure out a way to find a resolution, or should I say, find a way to win! We become immersed in our innate ability to be right; we conspire for our version to be right and true. (I remember reading somewhere that our version of a truth is indeed *only* a half truth... something to think about isn't it?)

Of course, when we internalise all of these emotions, we attract Hucha (toxic and heavy energy), which sticks to us like sand to a wet body. The more frustrated and disappointed we become, the more we attract the heavy energy.

This subsequently not only affects our relationships, but is the beginning of other areas in our lives going wrong. Our jobs become difficult; plumbing or heating systems in the house fail and cars break down. Even our immune systems start to weaken as we become more prone to colds and viruses. Eventually we may even start to experience stress-related illnesses. Humans are very adept at holding baggage like frustration, stress, anger and even guilt. The consequence of the internalisation is the effect on the physical and mental body.

If only we were able to sit down and discuss our grievances with our partners... maybe then, at that point, we would have brought in the Sami (light energy) into our souls and save ourselves all manner of future problems. But no... we always seem to do things the hard way, don't we?

Are we more likely to fight than find harmony?

Finding a Wholesome, Compassionate Solution

Finding harmony is finding a way to complement the differences. By this I mean finding a way to live with your partner (with both of you respecting each other) whilst also remembering the underlying fact that you are *both very* different.

Being in harmony could be like a chemical fusion. *Both* partners still maintain their *own* individual power, but by fusing the two together they become a *combined* strength which is wonderful. Then you will have achieved how to complement the differences. This is a very important concept in our Shamanic teachings, and it underlies much of our energy work.

Just like the two kinds of energy, Sami and Hucha, there are *two* stances within a relationship. There is the alliance between and the harmonising of the two different beings or energies.

Being in harmony does not necessarily mean being in balance, as balance is a dualistic term – where we so often seek to equalise two things; or make them the same. Remember, there are many flavours of energy. One is no better, more powerful or purer than the other. They are simply two expressions of the infinitely creative living energy.

There are, however, many expressions of these types of energy, including male and female. As we encounter different flavours of energy, we strive to recognise the distinctions between them, and to harmonise those differences, in order that these energetic differences are not obliterated, but celebrated.

We are all involved in countless energy exchanges every moment of our lives. To be aware of this, we have to know how our energies are forming or transforming the alliances between similar and dissimilar relations within our lives. (I know... that *is* a mouthful and much to get your head around).

Quite simply, all we need to do is to *appreciate* and *understand* that they are just different; and that you and your partner, even though committed to each other, are also different... even if only by gender.

Harmony is a place that we can operate from, in co-operation, rather than competition. All of us share these differences in our close relationships and with other individuals in our lives. If we are aware of these aspects and strive to harmonise these energetic interchanges, we can improve our interactions and communications with the other person and thus avoid accumulating Hucha (*toxic and heavy energy*) via arguments and frustration.

We can do this by simply *noting* the *similar* and *dissimilar* energies or incompatible energies that we are in contact with. We can then immediately assess the possible potential for creating or attracting Hucha.

What is different... is different!

What is similar... is similar!

However, we can seek points of alliance, work to harmonise the energies and thus lessen the chance of creating Hucha during arguments or frustration.

For further reading; see *Masters of the Living Energy, by Joan Parisi Wilcox.*

How Different are the Genders?

Other than the obvious (physical differences between the sexes), we also need to accept *both* the archetypal expectations of the role and the needs of each gender.

If you are feminine, please do *not* try to make your man feminine. The same goes for the masculine. We are both instinctively different beings; we think and do things differently to each other. It is time that we understand that and not ridicule those differences. Each sex deserves the same honour and respect that you would wish to receive.

Not only are we different in our emotions and thoughts, we are also dealing with something that the Qero calls: a 'similar and dissimilar energy force'.

Although the Qero term is a simpler way to understand what 'dissimilar' and 'similar' actually means, it is time to have a deeper understanding of this using a Western model....

It's All Down to Perception

NLP (Neuro Linguistic Programming), developed in the USA in the early 1970s, explores the relationship between how we think and how we communicate both verbally and non-verbally.

For example, when someone is describing an event it is not the absolute truth, but only the *perception* of the person describing that event. (Remember every truth contains only a half truth). This is down to either the association or disassociation one has to the event. Different people describe events differently to other people; it is usually in one of these three ways...

Either visually (what you see); auditory (what you hear); or kinaesthetically (what you feel).

Depending on which of the above is used, it will create a differing outcome. If a couple are engaged in an argument where the man is using his visual skills to inform his communication, and the woman on the other hand is using her kinaesthetic skills, the likely outcome will be different for both of them. Remember, his visual skill means that he is verbalising how *he sees* the facts, whilst her kinaesthetic reaction means she is verbalising how *she feels* about the facts; seeing versus emotion.

If one is seeing and the other is using emotions to solve a problem, this will most probably ensure that the outcome will take longer to resolve.

That is what is meant by being similar or dissimilar. If *both* communicated using visual skills, then the outcome would most likely be assured and the problem mutually resolved.

Neither is right and neither is wrong... just different.

When you find that you are battling wills with your partner or indeed anyone, especially when what you are both saying seems valid and right, remember, it is *not* a battleground where you try to bully the other into seeing *your* point of view. Because when different energies are battling wills against the other, it is almost impossible. This is definitely a situation where you will both have to agree to disagree, hopefully without any ensuing churlish sulks and silences.

Dissimilar and similar energy forces come into play in many areas of life; when dealing with work, friends or family members. How often have you watched a movie with other people and found that by the time you have talked about it there are *so many* differing accounts of exactly what happened in that film? This is all down to dissimilar and similar energies, or visual, auditory and kinaesthetic ways of seeing things.

We all seem to see and hear the same story, but just like in the game Chinese Whispers we all come out with a different version or interpretation of what we have seen, heard or felt about the story.

Imagine there are two women; they are sisters and constantly battling wills with each other. They end up slamming doors, crying, or even worse, resorting to 'fisticuffs'.

If you sat them both down and talked to them, you may possibly find that both of them are neither right nor wrong. What is at play here is perception.

One sister may *see* that the other is acting unreasonably; while the other is dealing with the information using her *emotions*. The interaction then becomes confused between *fact* and *emotion;* more than likely the outcome will be unresolved and confused, leaving both sisters angry or frustrated.

When this has been recognised, it is time to *step back* and recognise that some humans may not always see eye to eye, and that is *not* an invitation into the boxing ring. You just have to recognise it, that's all, and let it go... walk away... change the subject...

This is also a Global Problem

Looking at it from a worldwide perspective, ask yourself how many countries and cultures have an inability to be respectful to another's creed, colour or religion? How often do humans blatantly force their way into other countries?

We seem to do this because we do not agree with how other Governments are conducting themselves. We openly strip the power away, and barge our way in. We do it without even respecting that they have a different culture. According to us, they are just wrong: stupid... barbaric... heathen. That is our perception, not theirs.

We do not even *try* to understand that they may run things differently to us. As a consequence, what do we do; we waltz in, guns blazing and start a war. Iraq is a perfect example. You only have to read the history books to realise that humans are unreasonable, and really do like barging into other people's territories to steal and take.

What a fearful thought, if you think for one moment of how many lives have been lost, destroyed or changed, all because of one person's perspective of a given situation; Hitler, Bush and Blair to name a few. The Qero Elders have a much better ethos. They will recognise a difference in energy. They do this by using their energy body to 'taste' and ascertain the 'flavour' of that energy, all carried out without words or interaction.

If by tasting the energy they feel that it may be detrimental or toxic, they will walk away rather than collude or engage in a conversation. Their instinct warns them that the offending energy exchange would only result in an argument or even worse a fight.

Their ethos of not wasting energy exchanges seems to be very wise. After all, the first law of nature is that energy should always be conserved.

Communicating with Your Partner

If you feel that your partner is unhappy about something, try using these different techniques when communicating with them. Do this by firstly establishing the *facts* behind their unhappiness. Wade through any emotions that may ensue while the facts are being given and help by calming them down if the emotions do take over.

Remember, the facts should be heard by using your visual skills to see them *and* your auditory skills to help determine why they are so unhappy. *Both* of you should use auditory skills to resolve the issue, hopefully providing the unhappy partner with a visual conclusion and resolution.

So often we leave our loved ones alone to 'stew'; engrossed within their own thoughts; drowning in emotions that we seem to be frightened to get involved in, possibly due to a fear of opening up the proverbial 'can of worms'. That is very often *exactly* how relationships break down; through a lack of communication. It is all about quality communication...

People Change

The longer you have been in a relationship with your partner, the more likely it is that both of you will change.

As we get older our wants, needs and perceptions are likely to be different to when we were in our 20s. Just as aging changes our physical appearance, our minds also mature, so much so that even our personalities have been through an overhaul.

This affects *both* males and females as they head into their autumn years.

We change. Relationships change. Our outlooks change... *and* our love changes.

Chapter 8

Are we in Control, Controlling or Out of Control?

How often have you seen one of these terms become the mantle of a loved one, family member or colleague? In the present day you would be hard pushed not to recognise that many of us adopt at least one of these behaviours if only to survive and get through the day. Each one in its own right is a coping mechanism, which easily turns into a compulsive or obsessive disorder, and even though it is not recognised as a severe problem in modern society, too many of us are locked into the bind of having to be in control in some way or another.

When I first started writing about control, I thought it would become part of the Void Chapter. Then, as I began to think about it in greater detail, I was suddenly faced with the fact that this is a vast subject. Even though its legacy has an influence on many facets of our life, it could also influence several chapters within this book. For that reason alone, I felt that it needed rather more than just a mere discussion.

Therefore, join me for an in-depth exploration of how many of those terms in the title form the basis for several human conditions , especially when it involves the subject of the relationships we have with others or, more importantly, how we try to influence relationships with those around us (whether the relationship is with loved ones, partners, friends, family members or our working colleagues).

The pure and honest truth is that when watching certain people and how they interrelate with others, it is possible to see that their path of interaction is usually based on either learned practice or experience. We call this communicating from a place from which we are informed. (An informed place relates to our own personal bank of experiences that dictates how and why we communicate with others in the way we do).

This personal communication trait ensures that we employ a damage control tactic, thus saving ourselves from possible hurt or attack when involved in a situation where we are may be forced to defend ourselves.

Damage control literally means that we try to defend ourselves from our current vantage point. Often people use only their mortal intellect as their bank of experience. (The mortal intellect is the ego. The mortal intellect is our personality; it is fed by desire, thoughts, actions and deeds. It can become a beast, which growls and spits as it reacts to attack and challenge. Humans often deploy the services of the ego, rather than use intelligence when communicating with others. Intelligence is wisdom and is the flame of purification and truth, leading us out of the darkness of mortal intellect.)

This is the place that I would like to evaluate and understand as one can never be sure how much of a predicament one is in when one has to remain in control. This is probably due to the fact that one's emotions are so out of control that one has to become controlling purely to save face! Phew!

Let me throw this statement out there:

The mind is mad, and we all tread a fine line between maintaining our sanity and controlling our madness.

How often, during a possibly obsessive behavioural episode, have you thought some very irrational thoughts?

During those very private thoughts you have allowed them to become exaggerated by your intellect. Before you know it, the thoughts are then placed in such an order that they construct some very damaging sentences, all within the safe confines of your mind. For example, in a hypothetical situation in the workplace, you may be engaged in an argument with a colleague where to their face you say, 'Yes, I understand your viewpoint' while on the inside you are thinking, 'I wish this person would take a long walk off a short pier'.

Those internal thoughts are played with over and over, each formation more obscure than the last, until finally they start to play out as a mini soap opera set on the stage in the back of your mind.

Eventually, with little or no warning, they spring from the safety of your mind and come spewing out of your mouth as you give sound to each word! The conclusion being, of course, that it is inevitable that another human being is in your company, and they become the sounding stage for your irrational outburst. Meanwhile the person you are arguing with is struggling with their own thought processes.

Then throw this into the mix... the possibility that these thought processes are the result of an individual's seemingly out of control emotions. Have you ever walked down the street and noticed someone muttering to themselves?

Whether it is under their breath or out loud? You look on in amusement as you think: 'crikey what a nutter!' You then walk away with some sense of superiority, without even giving a thought to the many times that you too have been alone in your home or office and muttered something out loud to yourself! Honestly... you never have? Oh come on, I am sure you have at some point!

The truth is, of course, there are many times we have all done it! But is it a symptom of madness? I guess in some ways it is, especially if during your mutterings you ask yourself questions. Although a more measurable degree of madness only comes into play if you actually get an answer.

Now I really do not have a problem with accepting my own madness. I fully accept that we all have some element of it within us. I will let you decide whether the following proves it or not...

The Need for Control

What does it mean: 'To be in control'?

As you know, we are gifted with a marvellous imagination; do you remember those wonderful childish thoughts where your imagination was allowed to be creative? One minute you are conversing with your teddy bear, or flying over the ocean, the next, fighting with pirates, or being a fairy princess, perhaps even walking through the back of the wardrobe to a fantasy land, and sometimes talking out loud to an imaginary friend.

Then slowly, as you grew older, you were taught how to control that imaginative world; reigning in your imagination to keep these thoughts within the confines of your intellect, and to ensure that they never slipped out other than when you were alone, in case anyone would think you were mad!

From that moment on we are in the early grips of being taught how to control our thoughts and emotions. Remember how many times you were asked to stop crying? Even though you were feeling heartbroken and your body was involuntarily racked with sobbing, you would have to try to suck all of that unbridled emotion in, all in the name of controlling yourself.

Here again, we ask the question: Why do we need to be so in control? Is it purely to show the outside world how civilised we have become? Even now, when I read historical accounts about physical ailments of the Victorian age, I smile when I read about people who were classed as suffering from hysteria, or 'the vapours', or being classified as highly strung!

How about the vision of a rather frail Victorian lady from the upper classes who has just been told about her lover being lost in the jungles of Malaysia? She is seen holding her hand up to her brow and falling to the floor weeping hysterically! No one around her can soothe her, so she is whisked off to her room and placed in her bed until the doctor arrives and prescribes some 'calming powders'. Have you noticed in these accounts that there is rarely ever the option of talking or counselling?

I have often been with my own mother and heard her describe someone as highly strung. Once again, that sparked off thoughts of someone who was tied up tightly with a very taut binding material and how precariously that holds them until it snaps and they plummet to the floor and their imminent death!

I digress...

Does our fervent need to be in control become so important that we suffocate our true essence by placing such an impregnable jail around our souls? By doing this, do we forget that the fundamental requirement for human existence is based purely on experiencing the many facets of life? How many of us concentrate so intently on showing the outside world how much we can control our irrational thoughts and emotions, usually by closing off our sensory organs, so much so that we become cold and detached, closing off any attempts of experiencing life's rich tapestry?

Why is this? Well it's obvious because the alternative is to allow oneself to be out of control and this becomes a whole new ball game, one which many dare not experience.

When you are out of control, it paints a picture that one's emotions are spinning all over the place. The very thought of this strikes fear in the belly of those of us who love being in control.

In the early 1990s, I considered myself to be out of control. This was during a phase of experiencing very low self-esteem. I was tired a lot. I could not lose weight and I remember all manner of irrational thoughts taking over. In reality, I was in a place where I was out of harmony with myself. I was out of harmony with my mind, body and spirit.

During that time I experienced exactly how much my intellect had played tricks with me. My thoughts were like electric impulses running havoc inside my head. I remember at times feeling so confused with my emotions that I could almost feel that my mind was alive with chaotic moodlings. I struggled to be able to think of anything other than my inability to lose weight.

To my own detriment I began to control other areas of my life too, especially my work environment, it being the only thing I felt I could have control over. I became overly efficient. I was professional, well-organised, accurate and thorough. I was trusted to deliver. On the outside I was affable, gregarious, and congenial and always smiling, a seemingly professional and domestic goddess!

I remember a time when a friend of mine said to me: 'I bet you are nothing like you are at work when you are at home!' How true they were. The minute I returned home after being so in control for the past nine hours, I would crumble from the tiredness. My tension would consume me. I would often head straight for the breadbin or biscuit barrel and comfort-eat my way through my anxiety and confusion. This was my way of deadening those chaotic thoughts which plunged me to the depths of feeling out of control.

The price I paid for being out of control with my emotions and low self esteem, compared to my professional mask of competent control, was to exist as a polar opposite of who I really was. Truthfully I had lost sight of my essential self. I had lost 'Julie' in a sea of contradiction; this was to form the basis of my own personal healing journey.

What does it actually mean to you when you ask yourself the following questions?

I suggest you get a pen and paper and write down the answers, so that you can see them in print.

Do you feel that you are losing control?

How did you lose control?

Are you a controlling person?

Why are you controlling?

Do you need to control others?

Why do you need to control others?

Do you feel you are in control?

Do others control you?

Are your emotions and motives out of control?

If these questions are not recognised or handled appropriately at some point in our lives, we may then find ourselves facing a variety of ongoing problems or unresolved issues in the future.

Why Do We Need Control?

If we are in control of ourselves and our lives, perhaps this would then allow us to assume that everything we do or think is in complete harmony with ourselves and those around us. The definition of the word control means that our lives or events are manageable and organised; we are firmly in 'our own driving seat'; we make our own decisions; we choose where our lives take us; nobody else has any influence on how we are feeling.

Are you ready to go out and buy the t-shirt that has the words 'I can cope' on it?

Phew, what a wonderful blissful state that would be! How many of us can actually say that our lives are a statement of that fact? Hand on heart?

However, if that is the case for you, I admire you and you have done a great job with your personal evolution.

Just like me, you may, on the face of things, happily express that you are in control, when underneath the mask, there may be evidence of either being out of control, or that in some aspects of your life you are in the act of controlling. I would expect many people to have experienced an element of being out of control at some point or another in their life.

It is somewhat important to say here that some people feel they are perfectly in control of their lives, in some cases these people are more than likely to be suffering from the 'illusion of perfectionism', and that in itself can be a problem!

Being Out Of Control

Now, what happens when the unpredictability of life's events have pushed us on the road towards feeling out of control?

How do we then try to regain control, and in our attempt to do so reach for the void fillers as a means of calming ourselves down? Here, we are in the position of experiencing what it is like to feel out of control. If the feeling has been suffered and endured over several weeks, months or even years, it is likely that issues, people or events have nudged us way off of our 'harmony scale'.

It is also commonly true that another symptom of being out of control is the fact that we are being driven by other people, our home or working life, or by an event such as an emotional shock. Is it then that we try to reign in control of other things in our lives? Of course we do, after all it's self preservation. How do we do this? By becoming overly critical; by trying to attain perfection in the various things we encounter, whether that is an event we are planning or in the creation of a beautiful home that only stands as a show-palace; another mask. The aim is to distract any outside influences away from our chaotic inner persona.

Introduce me to someone who states that they are a perfectionist and I will say: 'It is not about perfectionism, it is about the overwhelming necessity for control'!

Pleasing Others

Very often, we are trying to please other people (and these can include a boss, parent or loved one). We are possibly doing this in an attempt to ensure that we remain in their grace, rather than show that we are flaky.

Subsequently, when our greatest fears are materialising, the chaos of the chatter within can develop into a possible mental illness, as we can only take so much of constantly trying to please others. Our chaotic state of mind will eventually and finally say: 'No more!'

Pleasing others is a 'coyote' type of character that we deploy (coyote is known as the 'trickster' in Native American power animals). Often as humans, we deploy the 'coyote role' in order to fudge over our real feelings or let on what is really going on inside. Many times, the reason that we are scared is that we fear we will lose the respect others have for us; we will squash the illusion we have created. Either way, it is a common human requisite that we are seen to be compliant and helpful, despite the fact that, deep underneath it all, we just want to scream out and tell those around us that we have had enough!

Controlling Others

How often do we try to control those around us, usually in a vain attempt to hide the fact that we ourselves are so out of control? Many of us will dispute this, as it is not a pleasant character trait, and one that none of us wants to admit to. More often than not, we do not even realise we are doing it.

Commonly, when something is not going the way we envisaged it (this could be either a relationship or an event), the first thing we do is to try to regain control; by whatever means! We will try whatever works: whining, nagging, chipping away, and if this does not succeed, we will resort to a control drama

The desired outcome is that we want to manipulate the loved one or event and thus create order from the chaos as we see it. Although the weird thing here is that no-one else sees it the same way.

Controlling other people is probably the most damaging behaviour we can engage in. This is mainly due to the methods used: whether it is whining, nagging, criticising or manipulation. You will most likely end up doing yourself no favours at all! Whether your loved one loves you unconditionally or not, by using these means you will eventually weaken the relationship or drive them far away from you.

We must all learn that, whether it is an inner lack of control, or the fact that we cannot stop ourselves from controlling others, it is imperative that we recognise what is going on within ourselves... and stop it!

Recognise that it is *you* that needs to heal the wound inside first. Then, and only then, can you regain your own power centre, ensuring that *you* firstly live *your* life in the best possible way that serves *you*.

Control Dramas

Just as I wrote about when we try to control others or an event, let us look at how we use a control drama to manipulate a situation.

Where does a control drama come from?

Well, it is lodged deep within your bank of experiences and it stems back to a time in your life when you could gain control of a situation by using various successful means.

What is a control drama?

It is a way of taking energy or control from another person by winning back power and scoring points, as it suggests. You find yourself using a tried and tested method in order to win back control of a situation that could potentially result in you being out of control.

For example, when you were a child and your sister or brother stole your toy, what did you do in order to get it back? Did you resort to screaming or crying? Did you resort to violence? Did you go and tell an adult who would retrieve it for you? If you were successful in using any of those methods, the very next time the toy was stolen or taken, would you not use the very same method that was successful the last time?

That is a control drama. Drama refers to the event surrounding the toy that had been taken. The control was the method used to get it back; scream, cry, hit, or get help.

Okay, let us try another one...

Imagine when you were younger, someone said something to hurt you. What method might you have used to control this drama? Refuse to talk to them? Argue with them?

Every child works out a different way to cope with a problem. We will all use differing methods, depending on our family dynamics. If you had several siblings then you may have used a method that would get the best attention, usually by either shouting or hitting. An only child may not have the ability or need to use those methods and may simply go off to their room quietly, choosing not to confront the problem.

Whatever method used, you will most likely employ the very same methods when you get older. That is how we work. You may have often heard someone say as an adult that his boss 'threw his toys out of the pram'; or a colleague 'took his/her ball away'. Both references relate to playground antics.

Even as we head into adulthood, we can use a control drama. How often have you had a disagreement with someone and used one of these two control dramas:

You find that you are not getting your own way; you refuse to talk to the other person and stay in the 'I'm not speaking to you' zone for hours or a few days until the other person apologises first?

Or, you find yourself backed into a corner and the only way out is to burst into tears. This is a classic control drama and used to deflect the attention away from being wrong or trying to make the other person pity you by feeling sorry for you.

For a better understanding of control dramas I recommend reading the book: 'The Celestine Prophecy' by James Redfield.

What is most important, however, is to realise that whatever method of control you use, or how controlling you can be, or how you employ a control drama in certain situations, it needs to be examined. It is time to check *yourself* when employing methods of control or manipulation. Do this by firstly looking into a mirror and asking 'Why am I out of control' or 'Why am I trying to control this situation or person?'

After this, engage in some self discovery of your own psyche and methods. Determine your reasons for employing the need for control in your life. What isn't working? Why are *you* feeling out of control?

It is important to make sure that you are firstly in harmony with yourself and in touch with your own emotions, especially before attempting to take another's power away, usually hidden under the guise of the word control.

More than likely it is *you* that is out of control and it is *you* that needs to ascertain why.

There is one alternative definitive solution, and it is rather radical... Go and try to live life as a hermit for a while, devoid of all contact with others. Escape the system, get out of the machine, go off grid and try and live a sustainable life!

Chapter 9

Shamanic Healing in Western Society

We are entrenched within a society that expects both the medical and pharmaceutical systems to cure all manner of physical and mental ills. We are terrified that if we seek alternative healing or help, then one of three things may happen: 1) we may waste our hard earned money in paying for such a service, 2) we may decide it is just too weird, untrustworthy and dark, or 3) we may discover it is all 'baloney'. We are unsure and often uninformed of the effectiveness of Shamanic healing because for some it is too strange and misunderstood.

If I am to take the mystery out of Shamanism, then this chapter in Shamanic healing will further explain and demystify what it is we do.

In Chapter 1, you have already had an insight into the basics of Shamanic practice, but let me take you deeper along the healing path, and explain in more detail…

Shamans practise different ranges of healing modalities, depending on their training and chosen core Shamanic path. As a trained Shaman who followed South American Core Shamanism, learning the practices of the Qero Indian from Peru, I can talk extensively on the modalities we use.

What is Shamanic Healing?

Alberto Villoldo of the Four Winds Society explains that…

It's important to differentiate between healing and curing. Curing is the business of medicine and has to do with eliminating symptoms. A cure will seldom ever result in a healing. Healing is a different business.

Healing works on four levels: the energetic; the mythic (the level of the soul); the psychological, where you can test out new beliefs; and the literal, where you can test out new behaviours, new diets, new yoga practices, new exercise routines.

We all know people who have been cured but who haven't been healed; they've had the tumour removed or worked through their mother issues, but they haven't changed their diet or eliminated life stressors. Or their interpersonal lives are a mess. Generally their symptoms will come back—six months, or a year, or six years later.

Have you heard the saying, 'If you change nothing, then nothing changes'?

If we are to evolve personally then we have to step fully into our healing path (Alberto Villoldo, *The Four Winds Society website*). We cannot simply rest back on our laurels and expect a healer to wave their magic wand, and 'hey presto'... we are cured. As Alberto says, 'Healing is different; healing is literally changing things that no longer serve us, whether that's physically, practically or energetically (or all three).'

What are the Things that No Longer Serve Us?

When you arrive at a point when you think that things cannot get any worse, or you have searched long and hard and been to see countless doctors, counsellors or indeed alternative practitioners, and even though there may be a slight improvement, that old emptiness or void in the pit of your stomach is still an uneasy place to linger.

Life's negative events, wounds, issues or bad experiences are all examples of the types of things that no longer serve us. There is an old saying about a man who walks the same street each day, and one day falls down a hole. Finally he gets out and the next day he does the same. On the third day what does he do? Does he take an alternative route or does he take the same old route, resulting in falling into that very same hole? The problem is when you find yourself repeating the same negative experience time after time (falling down the preverbal hole). The question is, how long does one keep repeating that before you decide to change something, and start your journey into wholeness?

How Does Healing Work?

Shamans work within the territory of the Energy body, commonly known as the Human Energy Field (HEF) or Luminous Energy Field (LEF), more commonly known as the 'aura'. This territory houses the energetic facets of the structure of the physical body, as well as our emotions, thoughts and feelings.

Knowledge of the HEF has been derived from ancient writings as well as metaphysical literature, but more commonly is it either perceived or seen by energy medicine practitioners. The HEF or LEF holds records of our personal and ancestral memories, negative life experiences and painful wounds (both present and past life). These experiences are known as imprints.

Imprints of physical trauma are stored in the outermost layer of the Luminous Energy Field. Emotional imprints are stored in the second layer, soul imprints in the third and spiritual imprints in the fourth and deepest layer.

Alberto Villoldo tells us that the Luminous Energy Field contains a template of how we live, how we age, how we heal and how we might die.

Humans need a positive flow of energy so that we can have the strength and vitality required for sustained physical or mental activity. Changes within our levels of energy can affect our physical and mental wellbeing.

Chakras

When we work within the HEF we also work within the major chakras.

Chakras are our energy centres (the major hubs) also known

as spinning wheels, funnels or vortexes. They are the openings where life energy can flow into and out of our HEF. Their function is to vitalise the physical body and to bring about the development of our self-consciousness. Chakras are associated with our physical, mental and emotional interactions. They are the major hubs of energy distribution, directing the energy to vitalise the nervous system, glands and ultimately all of the structures of the physical body. If our physical wellbeing is functioning efficiently then it is through our HEF that we are connected to everyone and everything that exists, the web of all living things.

There are between seven and nine major chakras and many minor ones, which are sometimes called meridians. These meridians are used by acupuncturists so that they can promote good energy flow throughout the human energy system. The minor chakras are influenced by action and physicality, but the major chakras deal with emotions and spirituality, as well as influencing your physical and mental health. When the physical or mental body is running low, or your HEF body is not functioning optimally, especially when affected with imprints, then the likely cause is often emotional or spiritual. Health concerns are attributed to an unbalanced chakra, which in turn manifests into a physical or mental ailment.

Each chakra relates to a specific part of the body and is again attributed to specific emotions and mental or spiritual problems; each one has its own vibration and colour.

The Human Blueprint

The Human Blueprint incorporates the Physical, Intuitive Intellectual, Emotional and Spiritual dimensions of human life also known as 'the whole'.

The basic spheres of existence are Quantum, Personal, Social, Global and External. The Personal sphere represents the self (inward focus). The Social sphere of life (outward focus) is about close relationships with family members, neighbours, friends, co-workers, spiritual family, and those with whom we come in contact on a regular basis. The Global sphere encompasses the Earth and all of humanity (upward focus). Beyond, and encompassing all of life, is the Eternal sphere. It is infinite, beyond space and time, and represents Spirit, the creative Source.

The human blueprint contains the information on our full potential; who we are, where we came from, and what we are here for. According to scientists our full potential is held encapsulated within our DNA, though much of that information is locked away in what is referred to as junk DNA. Modern Earth human DNA reportedly has genetic memories which are associated with the origins of humanity in the universe as part of a dispersal of over 130 billion human beings (according to Dr Michael Salla, of the American University Washington). Within this junk DNA there are around 223 genes which are literally unaccounted for and therefore untracked. Scientists reveal that therein lies the secrets of our origin. There are some Exo-scientists, includ DNA Nobel Prize winner Dr Francis Crick, who have discovered that some of that junk DNA comes from extra-terrestrials who have seeded part of their DNA in humans.

Within these 223 'junk' genes there are secrets that could unlock the human potential to shed our old energy body, which is shrouded in the density of human experience, burdened by our existence, relationships, fears and premature aging. The new energy body is a body which has been enlightened literally and figuratively. This will be a great transformation.

Dr Alberto Villoldo tells us that…

Through this great transformation, a new human is emerging on the Earth. I call this new human "homo luminous." Shamanic traditions understand that evolution happens within generations. In the West, we believe evolution happens in between generations: maybe your children will be smarter and more handsome; maybe the indigo children will climb to the next rung on the evolutionary ladder. The Shaman understands that evolution happens within generations. It is for us to take that quantum leap into who we are becoming. We can become homo luminous in our lifetime. This is our greatest task: to take these quantum leaps individually because as we do it for ourselves, we do it for the entire planet. Each and every one of us, when we choose truth, when we choose life, when we choose light, we are transforming the world.

The great transformation alters the normal route for our DNA, how we heal, age and die. The quantum leap allows us to grow new bodies, ones that heal, age and die differently. The great prophecies say that if we do not choose to evolve and if we don't take this quantum leap then mankind will succumb to The four horsemen of the apocalypse, which are Illness, War, Famine and Plague. The new human will have a new system which is resistant. The quantum leap of evolution ensures that we do not go down the same route of other species that haven't survived. 99 out of 100 species that have lived on this earth have perished.

If we choose to change the blueprint of our existence, then we have the ability to change the future which is predetermined for us.

How Can We Change Our Designated Blueprints?

The way to change the destiny which has been predetermined for us by our ancestors is to dream our own world into being. This means that instead of assuming the probable we assume the possible. If this sounds confusing then bringing it back to basics means that we choose change, and heal.

Remember that if we choose healing then we have to assume it on four levels, the energetic (soul level), the mythic (our story), the psychological (the mind) and the literal (physical). Now within each and every one of us lies the ability to do this. The role of the Shaman is to undergo the tracking and clearing of the imprints within the energetic level.

These imprints are like inactive computer files that reside within our energy bodies. When activated, they compel us towards certain behaviours, accidents and illnesses. These make up the stories of our woundings and negative life experiences. These stories are what make up the realm of the mythic. We narrate the story of our life's experiences, and the more we narrate it the more we hold onto the experience.

Imprints that are left unhealed orchestrate the repeat of incidents, experiences and the people we attract into our lives. For example, if you hold onto a wound of how your father left you when you were a child, this wound becomes an imprint, lying dormant, and you may wonder why you keep attracting certain men in your life who keep leaving you. This same imprint keeps on replaying until you heal the wound (connected to the story) of your father departing. Imprints propel us to re-create painful dramas and heart-breaking encounters that guide us towards situations wherein we can heal our soul wounds.

Colin Tipping, who wrote the book *Radical Forgiveness*, explains it really well:

Life is not just a random set of events without purpose or intelligence. What appears to happen haphazardly is really the unfolding of a divine plan that is totally purposeful in terms of our spiritual growth. We are co-creators with Spirit in the circumstances of our lives and we get precisely what we want (no exceptions). The extent to which we resist (judge) what we get, determines whether we experience it as either joyful or painful. Whenever we get upset with another person (or organisation), they are resonating in us something that we have condemned in ourselves and denied, repressed, and projected on to that person or thing. Our soul will always move us in the direction of healing and will keep on creating situations that offer us the opportunity to see the 'error' in our thinking or unconscious beliefs. People come into our lives to lovingly 'act out' the parts over and over until we heal the error.

The people who appear most troublesome are our greatest teachers, for they may be offering us the opportunity to heal by either mirroring what we have rejected in ourselves and projected on to others, or by forcing us to look at something we have repressed, or by keeping us on track with our mission (i.e. our agreement with Spirit to do certain things in our human experience to either meet a karmic debt, complete a past life contract, or assist in transforming energies within the human condition).

Shamanic healers will facilitate your healing journey using practices which can remove these imprints, and journey to establish a new contract; one which is free of karmic debt. Your healing journey will ensure that you won't have to keep replaying the same old wounded story, or keep meeting the same types of people, or be predisposed to the illnesses which affected your father and his father. Clearing an imprint from the HEF ensures that it ceases to be played over and over in our physical lives, therefore allowing you to dream your own world into being; one that is free of fate but one whereby you fulfil your destiny.

Chapter 10

De-Mystifying Shamanic Tools

A doctor uses a stethoscope, a nurse uses a syringe, the surgeon uses all manner of cutting devices and an orderly uses a trolley to transport the patients around. A Shaman is no different. He/she uses specific tools which will accomplish the job.

If you have visited a Shaman before, were you looking in anticipation at the many implements and incenses and paraphernalia that were placed around the space? Or if you haven't been to see a Shaman have you heard strange things about the tools we use?

This next chapter is going to place your mind at ease, as I simply and honourably debunk the myths and stories surrounding a Shaman and his/her tools.

You should by now be content that Shamanic practices are neither weird, strange nor cult like. In fact I remember one of my clients who came to me with a naivety concerning the knowledge of Shamanic practices. After a few visits, I was explaining about energy and the beliefs we have. Out of the blue he asked me; 'I don't really know what to believe or understand about Shamanism, is it a cult?' I answer the same to you as I did my client: No, Shamans are not involved in any way in cults or the activities of cults.

Why Do We Use Tools?

A Shaman uses tools for the same reason anyone uses tools, because of their effectiveness in helping one do a job effectively. For a Shaman there are a few reasons; practicality (meaning using the appropriate tool for a specific part of a healing) and ceremonial (which refers to using either a rattle or drum or incense in ceremony), and for some there is even showmanship. For me it is both practical and ceremonial.

The use of Shamanic tools helps a Shaman focus and express energy received from Spirit, the Web of Life and individuals. They are a basic requirement when embarking on the Shamanic path and are used for healing, diagnosis, cleansing, journeying and divination.

The Shaman uses many tools for both ceremonial and healing work. Respect and reverence are the essential virtues needed to work with such sacred implements, and it is only by coming from a place of purity and an open heart that one can be brought into alignment and further expansion with the physical, mental, emotional and spiritual realms.

Shamanic Tools

A lot of Shamanic work involves ceremony (there will be more information later on in another chapter on ceremony). The tools Shamans use are part of the respect and credence for their part in ceremonial work. A prime example of ceremony is paying respect to the Earth, directions and cosmos, and this is shown perfectly when a Shaman opens 'sacred space'.

Sacred space is a healing sphere; a space which is safe and pure. When we open sacred space we create a connection to the Divine and can summon the healing power from nature or the luminous ones, those ancient medicine men and women from the spirit world.

In Western culture much of our fear and pain is drawn from the feeling that the world is not a safe place for us. Within sacred space everyone is protected. By opening sacred space we leave behind all manner of ordinary reality and life, exchanging it with a space where we can meet and commune with the Divine in all things. It is a space which allows us to enter the quiet of non-reality to find healing and wisdom. Within this space our problems become lighter and we are literally and gently touched by the hand of spirit.

A Prayer to Open Space

Stand and face each geographical direction as you say the prayer; touch the Earth for Mother Nature; hold hands aloft for Father Sky…

Winds of the South, great serpent… help me to shed the past the way you shed your skin, all in one go; with good intention and mindfulness of my task.

Help me to walk in Beauty and Grace.

Winds of the West, jaguar, and queen of the jungle… protect this medicine space; show me the way beyond fear and give me the courage I need for my task. Help me to release any heaviness.

Help me to walk in Beauty and Grace.

Winds of the North, hummingbird, little bird of joy… protect me on my 'epic journey'; show me how to drink directly from the nectar of life. Help me to walk in Beauty and Grace.

Winds of the East, eagle/condor, and great bird of prey… show me how to soar high above all pettiness; allow me to fly wing to wing with Great Spirit.

Help me to walk in Beauty and Grace.

Mother Nature, Mother Earth… although you sustain me daily, please help to ground me; allow me to walk on your belly with respect and with honour.

Help me to walk in Beauty and Grace.

Father Sky, to the Star Nations, Sister Moon, to Great Spirit… you who are known by many names to many people; be with me here now as I walk along this fragile road.

Help me to walk in Beauty and Grace.

When you have finished your healing work or meditation, it's advisable to close sacred space.

Prayer to Close Sacred Space

Use this prayer to close down the sacred environment after you have finished your desired work.

Winds of the South, great serpent... thank you for helping me to walk in Beauty and Grace.

Winds of the West, jaguar, queen of the jungle... thank you for helping me to walk in Beauty and Grace.

Winds of the North, hummingbird, little bird of joy... thank you for helping me to walk in Beauty and Grace.

Winds of the East, great bird of prey... thank you for helping me to walk in Beauty and Grace.

Mother Nature, Mother Earth... thank you for helping me to walk in Beauty and Grace.

Father Sky, the Star Nations, Sister Moon, Great Spirit... thank you for helping me to walk in Beauty and Grace.

In order for Shamans to do their work they must first effect a change of consciousness within themselves. The Shaman enters into an ecstatic state, depending on the Shaman's intention, which could be to journey or it could be ceremonial. The state is entered either hypnotically or through the use of a plant-based hallucinogen, during which time they are said to be in contact with the spirit world, and to enter a separate reality.

Some of the methods for affecting this consciousness shift are:

- Drumming or rattling
- Fasting
- Sweat lodge
- Vision quests
- Dancing or spinning
- Use of 'power plants' such as tobacco
- San Pedro, named thus (St. Peter) by Andean natives because he's the guardian of the Gates of Heaven
- Ayahuasca Quechua or 'Vine of the Dead'

Tools and Their Uses
Drums

The drum can have a variety of uses; it can be used to cleanse a space which is holding onto negativity or heavy energy, or it can beat a rhythmic beat in fire ceremonies or for Shamanic journeying. A drum's beat should mirror the slow deep beat of the Mother Earth. The drum, like a rattle, acts like a metaphorical spirit horse on which a Shaman rides into other dimensions to gain answers for healing and problem solving. The beating of the drum enables the Shaman to enter into a conscious shift.

Rattles

These are used for opening and creating a sacred space, or they can ascertain a diagnosis for a client. By the way the sound changes, the rattle can determine the presence of heavy or negative energy. It can also be used to unwind the chakras or to dislodge toxic sludge from the HEF.

Feathers

Feathers are used to assimilate the element of air, which is used to cleanse and smudge a client's HEF, or a room. The feather is used as a way to transfer the smoke from smudging herbs as deep gratitude and thanks to spirit.

Pendulums

Pendulums are one of the easiest and most accurate of the divining tools. They come in many different styles; from a suspended crystal point to a ring placed on a string. Their uses are as a response to questions, or as an indication that a chakra is unbalanced and not functioning correctly.

Smudging and Spritzing Herbs

The use of the smoke from incense and herbs is classic in Shamanic practices. The type of herbs can range from White Sage,

Sweet Grass, Copal, Palo Santo, Agua de Florida Water and many more. When a Shaman uses smudging or spritzing, it can be for cleaning and protecting purposes, to remove toxic sludge or heavy energy, for opening space, or as gratitude and thanks to Spirit. The method of spritzing is often used in opening space as it is said that the act alone is a direct gift from the soul of the Shaman, as the breath comes from the belly and heart centres.

Tools You Can Use
Space and Body Cleansing

Living in this fast-paced materialistic society creates disharmonious human beings. People become obsessed with wants, greed, power or are just plain unhappy. Today, it is so important to keep our home and physical bodies clear of any *negativity* that may accumulate. Otherwise, negativity creates imbalance within our physical systems as well as between people. Humans can attract negativity in many ways; we are the ONLY species that does this.

Example

One only has to go out shopping in a busy retail centre during Christmas or the sales to know how drained you can get. If you imagine 500 plus people, all walking around the same space, breathing in the same air, with literally millions of things going on in their heads, trying to make their way from shop to shop; getting frustrated with the heat and crowds; perhaps worrying about the money they are spending... it is no wonder that you arrive back home exhausted.

The reason for this is that your energy body is attracting all of that negativity that is being bandied around and it ends up sticking to you like tar. Even being in the presence of a heavy or heated discussion with someone will result in attracting it.

Our homes can be affected too, even if it may have been inadvertently created by years and years of hoarding; dust is one of the main culprits of holding stagnant negativity. It may be due to the people in your home creating it by having unhealthy communications with each other, for example; arguments and toxic thoughts, certain types of TV programmes that we watch (like the news or violent films). These create an unhealthy balance of negativity that just wafts around...

Sometimes houses can also carry and hold negativity from their previous owners, either living or deceased. Believe me, it can take hold like a 'heavy smog'. *That* is very hard to escape from! This really does need to be cleared regularly.

Here are a few guidelines. (Of course, you could hire a professional space clearer who would clear your home of any negativity; some are also skilled in moving on restless spirits).

Cleansing the Physical Body
General Cleansing

- Buy some white sage leaf (available from all good holistic shops) and a fire-proof dish.
- Find a quiet space for about five minutes. Light the sage. As the flame goes out smudge yourself with the smoke: ensure that the smoke wafts over your whole body, back and front; paying attention to bringing it into the front of your body around your chakras. These are located at the base of the spine, stomach, solar plexus, heart, throat, middle of your forehead, and on the top of your head.
- Sit quietly after you have finished. Imagine a clear crystalline light entering into the top of your head. Visualise drawing it down through the inside of your body, clearing and cleansing all the way down to your feet. Then pull the light over the outside of your body until it reaches the top of your head again. Spend a few minutes bathing in the crystalline whiteness, imagining any heaviness being eradicated and turned into light. Gently come to, slowly get up and breathe deeply in and out a couple of times.

Heavy Cleansing (After Arguments)

- Get hold of some Agua de Florida Water (Peruvian), available from Shamanic shops; or some frankincense incense.

- For the Florida Water: Place it in an atomiser. Then, in a quiet place, spray it around the outside of your energy body or aura, back and front. Spray a little over the heart chakra and at the same location on your back. (This will help clear any personal attack that you may have been a victim of).

- For the frankincense: Light the taper and wait until the flame dies and you are left with just smoke. Then, as with the Florida Water, smudge yourself around the exact same areas, ensuring you also do your heart chakra, back and front.

- Repeat the last step of general cleansing; sit quietly and imagine the clear crystalline light clearing and cleansing your body.

You can also carry out this cleansing for other members of your family that may have been affected by attracting negativity from a bad encounter or an argument. The importance here is to make sure that *all* members of your family join in this practice, thus ensuring that your home does not accumulate this toxic energy.

House Cleansing

Your home should be cleared about every three-six months to ensure that positivity and flow is encouraged. This involves *all* rooms in the home being cleansed; including bathrooms and toilets as well as the garden.

You will need to buy or get hold of the following items: Californian White Sage and a fireproof bowl; Tibetan bells, or you can use your hands by clapping them; juniper oil and a small dish with water in; lavender oil and an oil burner; a small candle and matches.

Prepare all the items in readiness on a tray that can easily be carried from room to room.

- Firstly, clean the house, so that it is free of dust and clutter (don't think you have to spring clean it! You just need to dust, vacuum and tidy any visible clutter.)
- Place 10 drops of juniper oil into the dish with water in and place on the tray.
- Light the candle and take it with you to light the sage when needed.
- Go around each room of the house in a *clockwise* direction.
- Enter the first room; first light the sage and then use the smoke to smudge the whole room. Make sure that *all* corners and doorways are smudged.
- Then go around the same room with the Tibetan bells or clapping and move the energy around using the sound of the item chosen. If you are using your hands then clap around the room. The idea here is to use sound to dispel any negative energy.
- With the juniper oil and water mixture, use your fingers to spread a few drops into each room.
- Repeat this for every room in the house. Pay particular attention to bathrooms and toilets.
- When the entire house has been cleared you will really notice the difference. Place some of the lavender in the burner (around 10 drops) and place the burner in the hallway. Let the aroma spread throughout the entire house.
- Discard any used sage and juniper oil into the Earth.
- Try to keep fresh flowers in the hallway each week; or perhaps light a candle now and again (be very safe with any lit candles!)
- If you feel that someone or the house itself is experiencing a particular 'toxic attack' by someone please do call in a

space clearing professional. They will happily give you advice and/or clear the space for you.

- Using sea salt to clear heavy energy: get hold of some larger granules of sea salt. Create a perimeter of salt around the whole of your property, ensuring to place a line of it at each doorway into the house. Salt is a great emulsifier of negativity! If you feel that you are personally under attack then have a sea salt bath. Maybe put some juniper or frankincense oil in as well. This will help to ensure proper cleansing and protection.

The Use of Sand Paintings

Sand paintings have been created by the North and South American Indians for centuries. They can be used for healing or blessings.

When a sand painting is created it becomes a place where 'the gods come and go'. It is a medium where you can put an issue to the mythic and let spirit help you with it. The sand painting is a crucial element in helping one move forward from a blockage; it can restore balance thus restoring lost health or ensuring 'good things'. A sand painting is usually completed in one day and destroyed the next day.

Regardless of the sand painting's origin, one fact is clear: it is transitory, a specific rendering of a sacred art form that is destroyed the next day. Therefore, there is no pictorial evidence of what sand paintings looked like hundreds of years ago. Our only clues lie within the records of 'kiva' walls, cave walls and mural fragments from several hundred years ago.

The Role of Sand Painting

Sand paintings can be constructed to balance something within you that is out of balance. They can be as simple or elaborate as you wish. A Navajo medicine man would simply draw in the sand the person who was ill, leaving the image until the next day and then destroying it.

Today they are not always called sand paintings, but nature paintings. They can be constructed outside, somewhere private, using any items found in nature.

You construct them because you want to *move forward* from a debilitating issue; or you require some help with a question. It really is all about artistic licence.

Construct one to honour the fact that you have completed some healing or because you have finally let go of a long-standing issue. Traditionally, sand paintings are created and left overnight. The desired effect may not manifest itself in a day, but it is the construction and knowledge that is important.

Suggestions for materials:

- Grasses
- Flowers (first ask permission from the plant)
- Sticks
- Acorns
- Herbs
- Feathers
- Stones

Construction of Sand or Nature Paintings

Pick a quiet area in your garden; a wood; a field or beach somewhere that you can easily get to.

- Pick a spot that you feel safe in.
- Open Sacred Space, using the prayer mentioned earlier.
- With the issue or problem in mind, walk around the area picking up the materials that you require for the construction of your painting.
- Take the material back to your chosen spot. Construct a circle that will protect the painting; use anything as the

circular border, such as stones, wood or grasses.

- With the *intention* of the problem in your mind, create a design within the circle, blowing the *intention* into each piece of material before you place it in its spot.

- The importance is that you use your *intention* with the problem in mind when you place down each object.

- When the design has been completed (it doesn't have to be a piece of well-known art), spend a few minutes with your finished painting. Place your hands inside the circle. Ask the universe or Mother Earth to help you to sort this problem out.

- Leave the sand painting, which you will return to the following day, or maybe even the day after.

- When you return, sit with the painting and with the problem in mind. See how you now feel about the initial problem. Do you think or feel differently? Has the problem's hold on you lessened in any way? Do you feel that you now have more clarity?

- If you feel the *same* as you did before you constructed the painting, then look again at your design and see what has changed. What does it look like now? If you feel that more work on the painting is needed, then add something or change something that will urge a stronger energy connection. Then leave it again for one or two nights.

- When you return again you may not be able to decipher the result. Don't worry about this, as the important thing here is that you 'gave it to spirit' and the outcome will be whatever is right!

- When you feel that your sand painting has done all it can (this may not be the end as you may not feel that you have been helped at all), please remember, these designs work deep within the subconscious part of us, subtly changing the heaviness of the energy that is related to your problem.

Please Note: These are very powerful tools that *always* work, whether it is either a subtle or intense change in energy. Remember to deconstruct the design, leaving no trace of it whatsoever. Close Sacred Space and leave.

An Everyday Tool – The 'Take-it-Away' Box

If constructing a sand painting is a little too 'wacky' for you to even contemplate, there is a modern tool that can also be used, for single or family people alike. It is called the 'Take-it-Away Box'.

This may be used in the same way as you would a sand painting. Once again, the essence here is to try and sort out a problem that you simply cannot find a solution to. Occasionally they are used in families when a compromise cannot be reached specifically with issues relating to the children or a spouse.

First, you will need to get hold of a box; a small cardboard box will do. Glue all of the sides together so that no-one can retrieve anything from it. If you wish, you can decorate it. Cut a postal size slot in the top, big enough to place a piece of paper through.

Please make sure that everyone in the household knows that it is a 'Take-it-Away Box'.

How to Use It

When there seems to be an irresolvable issue or disagreement, then get the person/s involved to write down the problem or issue on a piece of paper. Blow into the paper the requirement to give the problem away and simply place the paper in the box and forget about it!

Over time, the box may become full. When this happens, simply take the box outside and safely burn it, complete with all of its contents!

Then make another one to use.

Chapter 11

Ceremony – Creating the Authentic Relationship

It is important to include a chapter on ceremony and ritual, because by execution alone it allows us to be more present, as it focuses the mind on much more sacred and vital practices. For many of us in Western society, ceremony teaches us to slow down, be patient and most of all it teaches us trust.

When you hear the word ceremony I suspect there are some of you who will roll your eyes in exasperation. As often it conjures up a vision of spending long hours in a state of silence, while a vicar or priest performs ritual, prayer and goodness knows what else. Unfortunately now in Western society ceremony is often only practiced by organised religion, and for some the closest we get to participating in a ceremony is likely to be a wedding, christening or a funeral.

The modern man's awareness of ceremony is indeed limited, but what we fail to realise is that creating and taking part in ceremony is like 'coming home' back into the loving arms of the sacred, Mother Earth and the Divine. It is a place of complete connection and a way of basking in the beauty of an authentic relationship.

Today, in the West, so many have lost connection with the very Earth we live on. In fact, some of us are so disconnected and lost within our busy schedules and routines (which become the mainstay of our work and social lives) that the closest we get to a ritualistic act is nothing more than lighting a cigarette, or the ritual of drinking coffee. Many of us have even lost the ability to be still and quiet for a moment, possibly because some are fearful of what the silence holds.

What sets apart Western and native cultures is quite simply the ability to perform ceremony and ritual.

Indigenous cultures have always had a conscious relationship with the land they inhabit, and in the past many had sustainable cultures which often lasted for thousands of years. They also had a rich ceremonial and ritual life. A ceremonial ritual can be as simplistic as a blessing and giving thanks for the food you have been offered to eat, or as complex as the ceremony conducted in a Catholic Mass. It doesn't matter what your beliefs are, there is always a place for ceremony in your life. Simple rituals provide us with moments of sheer quiet and offer a sense of blissful peace and a chance to meet the sacred in all life. It's like taking a holiday away from those busy routines.

Taking part in or creating one's own ritual or ceremony allows one to connect at a deep level. It is a way to enter into dialogue with the sacred, or Great Spirit or the Divine; whatever your belief or figure head is. Because there are thousands of people from all over the world who have turned their backs on religion, many are even more reluctant to create a focal point of reflection, whether that is a sacred space within the home, or a place of tranquillity in the garden. Even those two creations alone would open a portal of connection with the Divine, offering untold peace and space to breathe, pray or just be.

Creating Ceremony

There are many reasons to create a ceremony, whether it's for celebration, change, connection or to honour the completion of something. A simple act of lighting a candle and holding the required intention in mind is ceremony in its simplicity.

Shamans love ceremony! Any excuse to enter into a sacred dialogue or spend a blissful time in peace and reflection... then we are there. The place that most of our ceremonies are conducted is usually around a fire, which is one of the most natural yet ancient of things.

Fire Ceremony

Working with fire is a very powerful way of celebrating change or releasing something that doesn't serve you. Many who join us around a fire come with an intention and a need to release something, to honour or to invite something positive into their lives. Fire is very healing and transformational.

Fire ceremony is one of the most wonderful tools that we can use when we really want to experience the power of letting go of an issue or problem. It is exceptionally powerful as well as cathartic in its execution. There is nothing more powerful than standing around a fire that you have built and set light to, a fire that you have placed your problems in, and watched as the flames consume them, transforming the heavy energy accumulated around the problem, seeing it change into light energy infused from the living flame as it is consumed. It is so amazingly powerful and invigorating!

As you enter such peace, you feel the warmth of the fire, your mind letting go of the issues that have caused you so much pain. In those wondrous moments you suddenly feel transported back in time, a time when you can remember sitting around a fire with your tribe and its elders; a sense of safety and belonging takes over... and it is at that precise moment that you *know* that everything will be just fine!

A fire ceremony can be conducted on your own or with others that you would like to share the experience with.

Preparing for Fire Ceremony

ALWAYS light your fire outdoors and in an area that is a safe distance away from trees, fences or any homes.

Procedure

- Collect together newspapers, matches and some white sage.
- Take some olive oil to bless the fire with.

- Construct the fire using the newspapers, straw (if you can find it) and dry wood. Ensure you place the paper and straw on first; then build a small pyramid with the wood. Create a fire that is manageable and that you are happy with (big is not always better)!
- Walk around the garden and collect some small sticks that will be used to represent your problem(s) or issue(s); or use sticks that you have already collected from the woods prior to the ceremony. (Remember you can place as many problems or issues on the fire as you need).
- Use the prayer to open Sacred Space.
- Light the fire.
- As the flames start to grab hold, pour on the olive oil in small amounts three times (spacing each one out over 10 minutes). This is to bless the fire, and it is your way of honouring the fire ceremony. Blow into the white sage, using your intention of breath to infuse the sage. This is to give thanks and blessing to spirit.
- Wait until the flames die down from roaring to a healthy burning ember.
- When it is safe, approach the fire with your sticks, sitting down. Take each stick in turn (keeping one back for a blessing for others), then use your breath to blow into the stick the issue or problem that you wish to rid yourself of. Then place the stick into the burning embers and watch the flames consume it. Do this with each stick in turn.
- When all of your issues and problems have been consumed, take the stick that you kept back and use it to pass on a blessing for either a loved one, a sick friend or use it for a global blessing. Then place this stick on the fire to burn.
- When all of the sticks have gone, place your hands at a safe distance over the top of the fire (don't burn yourself). Bring the heat or smoke firstly into your stomach area; then your

heart area; then lastly into your forehead area. You are doing this to replace all of the heavy energy that has been accumulated in your body whilst holding onto the problem, with light (Sami) energy.

- Sit with the fire for as long as you wish, relaxing, meditating or just enjoying the experience. Feel the ancestors as they come and sit alongside you. Feel how connected you feel. Above all, feel the peace as it enters your physical body.
- When the fire is almost out, use the prayer to close Sacred Space.

The fire ceremony usually takes about two weeks to transform and change your perception relating to the problem(s) or issue(s). During that time you may feel a detachment from it or you may experience other rumblings inside of you that relate to other issues; issues that may have been long forgotten or buried. If they do arise, let them pass through your mind without analysing them too much. It is all part of the fire ceremony's healing process.

If any of these rumblings cause you too much upset or distress, go and visit a reputable Shamanic Ppractitioner for further healing and guidance.

Creating an Ancestral Altar or Space in Your Home

If you would like to do something to honour your ancestors, I have a suggestion…

Try setting up a quiet place somewhere in your home, preferably situated in a northerly direction (ancestors are linked to the North direction in the Peruvian Medicine Wheel tradition). Here, set up a small table or use an existing shelf. On this you can place photographs of your ancestors, as many as you wish to place. If you do not have a photograph of a certain relative, then place an object that is either closely connected to them or is linked to a known pastime or character trait of theirs.

Maybe, every now and then, place fresh flowers on the altar. Keep a candle there. Use any other objects that you feel appropriate. Once in a while, when you feel the time is right, spend some quiet time in this area. Remember your ancestors; remember their funny or serious ways; remember what they did in their lifetimes... and honour that.

You may of course, have an ancestor that in your view has not acted too honourably during their time on Earth. If that is the case, then it is still okay to have them represented. Honour their life too, and don't forget, they still had a part to play in your life! It is okay to honour them. That does not mean that you have to be in agreement with how they decided to spend their lifetime.

Remember, they *also* need light sent to them to help illuminate their darkness.

Spend quiet times within this ancestral place. Use it to connect to the ancestors. Use quiet moments or meditation to ask for gifts from them; maybe an answer to a question, or a quality you may need.

On the anniversary of their deaths, as well as placing flowers on the grave, maybe light a candle for them. Remember to send love, light or forgiveness to them. It is a lovely feeling, as you really can connect to them and you no longer have to feel that they have left you in a void. Surely this is a much better way to honour their passing than just remembering them as ashes or in the coldness of a grave.

I genuinely feel that using our hearts and our memories to remember the deceased is far more beautiful than an obligation to tend their graveside, which sometimes tends to become more of a chore than an honouring.

Lastly

Remember that the beauty of creating ceremony is as a way to connect. It's a way to sit in a blissful space and pray, or it's a way to ask Great Spirit for help and guidance. Even learning to meditate is a cathartic action which creates a bridge between the physical and non-physical, accessing the higher realms.

The lack of ceremony and the ability to celebrate any rites of passage is something we have forgotten in our culture. The mere action of celebrating puberty, or the onset of a girl's first menses, realigns us all with the sacred action of celebration, as well as supporting an individual as they take possession of their own unique gifts and potential. Celebrating and honouring a milestone in someone's life affords them a unique ability to leave the old behind, so that they walk forward into a new stage of their life, free of the old ties that bind them.

Chapter 12

The Alchemical Process of Transformation

For so many of us the mere sound of the word transformation is both a mystical and unattainable process. We often feel that it is impossible to be able to change our current mode of being, let alone transform ourselves from being fixated with our ailment, fear or anger. Surely transformation is for those who have undergone an epiphany or life-threatening event... or is it?

Whenever I use the word 'Alchemy' I know it sends an uncontainable shiver up many people's spines. That's because it is one of those words which sparks off a sequence of ripples within the energy body. It awakens the soul's calling and urges us to take notice that it's time to heal or to become aware. The soul knows this ancient word well, but the ego mind is fearful of it. This is because the moment the word is spoken the ego mind goes into a blind panic as it tries to save itself from going through any unnecessary upheaval, even though it stealthily comes in the guise of healing, and it's a nudge that it's time to let go of the wounds we hold.

I love to use this word because to me healing is an alchemical process; it is one of transmutation and transformation. In the past and present, alchemy is a process that many chemists have been striving to do and that is to transform a base metal into gold. It also means that we change or transmute the lead of our personality into the gold of our becoming. On the basis of that, surely that's a good thing, especially if we believe our lives should be spent living sacredly as well as the chance to learn and evolve? The only way to attain illumination is to walk along the path of the wounded with an objective to becoming whole again.

Principles of Life

For those of you who follow the Bible's creed of the Ten Commandments (a list of religious and moral laws that according to the Abrahamic religions were given by God to the people of Israel from Mount Sinai) you may not be aware of another list of principles which are ancient in their origin. They are known as The Kybalion. Even though the book was published much later in 1908, the origins possibly predate Christianity. The seven principles stated in the Kybalion were purported to be principles of life written by Hermes Trismegistus, who was not only deemed to be a wise pagan priest but also an ancient Hellenistic combination of the Greek God Hermes and the Egyptian God Thoth, known for both writing and magic.

Why do I find his writings fascinating? It has to do with those great principles of life which to me are the basis of living our lives both in a sacred way and as a guide for healing our wounds. I also believe that the ancients not only had a great knowledge of our human purpose on this Earth, but they also knew that we would be faced with many challenges. That is why these ancient texts were written. The Kybalion was written as a guide for those challenging times. The only trouble they possibly didn't foresee is the unequivocal onslaught of organised religions, which have somewhat squashed and buried these ancients texts, therefore keeping humans shackled to those mainstream doctrines, fearful that we may evolve beyond our status.

The Kybalion

These seven principles of life are enlightening and I feel that they can benefit our lives now as we continue living within our western civilisations. They are not complicated and for those of you who wish to find your authentic self, or are seeking a healing path (or if you are just fascinated with Shamanism) then this is another great tool. It can also form the basis of discussion and thought.

Bearing in mind I have stated that healing is an alchemical process, let's look at the Kybalion as a mental process, one of the four levels required in a Shamanic healing modality. The Kybalion is geared around mental transmutation which is the art of mental chemistry wherein an individual changes and transforms his own mental states and conditions, an ancient form of NLP (Neuro Linguistic Programming), as practical today as it was thousands of years ago, just like Shamanism.

Here is a brief explanation of those principles, written to help you understand them on a fundamental level.

One: The Principle of Mentalism

Everything is 'the mind'; the mind is all. It includes the material universe, life, matter and energy. Everything we create as humans is in the mind. In Shamanic terms everything is alive and is connected to everything else by an invisible web. The principle of Mentalism underpins that by saying that everything in our inner realities, as well as our outward manifestations, are one of the same and as it is contained within our own universes (our mind). As a microcosm it is contained within the mind of the 'All' (the macrocosm), which contains all of the many universes. All life, and the Earth, is all in the mind of the Divine. One of the old Hermetic Masters wrote, long ago: 'He who grasps the truth of the Mental Nature of the Universe is well advanced on The Path to Mastery.' These words are as true today as at the time they were first written.

Two: The Principle of Correspondence

There is an association between the various planes of existence of being and life. The principal as above, so below is overriding here. The principle states that there is harmony, accord and association between the planes of The Physical, The Mental, and The Spiritual.

Three: The Principle of Vibration

Everything in the universe, both the microcosm and macrocosm, vibrates at a constant and steady rate. Everything has motion, from the highest vibration of the Divine to the lowest vibration of matter, and everything moves, vibrates and circles. Even our thoughts, emotions and desires vibrate at differing rates, each one attracting similarly matching experiences. Vibration is the start of the transmutation process of changing one's own mental state, and we do this by using our own effort to direct and change our individual will, by amplifying and radiating positive thoughts.

Four: The Principle of Polarity

Everything is dual. There are two sides to the scale, and everything has an opposite. Where there is life the opposite of this scale is death. Where there is good health, the opposite is sickness, and where there is richness there is poverty. This principle states that everything is and isn't at the same time. Some humans have a tendency to place themselves at differing points of a scale, some at the extremes, and others coasting along in the midway point where it neither is nor isn't. It just teeters and waits at the place where there are truths and half truths at the same time.

Five: The Principle of Rhythm

In everything there is reciprocal act; a measured motion; a swing backward and forward; a pendulum-like association. Within the principle of polarity there is rhythm between one pole and another. Even our bewildering states of moods, feelings and emotions are due to the to and fro of the pendulum. This principle states that the swing is always towards one side of the pole and then to the other. Therefore there is always an action and a reaction, an advance and a retreat. Rhythm ensures that night follows day, and day follows night.

Six: The Principle of Cause and Effect

Nothing happens by chance. Everything in the universe has an identifiable cause. Chance relates to an obscure cause that we cannot perceive or understand. It is a cause that hasn't happened yet. Causes are not the creations of events or circumstances, they are catalysts of a long line of them, usually driven by the underlying beliefs of life.

Seven: The Principle of Gender

Gender is a coalition between the masculine and the feminine, but not in the sense of procreation or different sexes. The Kybalion states that gender exists on all the places of existence (physical, mental and spiritual) representing differing aspects on the different planes.

Masculine energy sends its energy out into the world, and the feminine energy is receptive and attracting. Masculine energy is expressed in the conscious mind and the feminine is expressed in the unconscious mind.

The principle of 'ME' is the feminine embodying our moods, mental states, our habits and our body. The principle of 'I' is the masculine which embodies our wishes, desires and intentions. The 'I' calls the 'ME' to act. To put this simply, the feminine is receptive and creates the ideas that the masculine puts into action.

How on Earth do you use all of this information for your own physical, mental and spiritual wellbeing?

There is a principle for healing which allows one to change or transform the self and free itself from the wounds and negative life experiences it has endured. Remember before I mentioned your free will, the ability to freely choose the path one walks in their life? Well, if you remember that free will has to fit in with your own personal circumstances and ability to be able to freely choose, then the ability to find the healing path that suits you will depend on certain factors.

Shamanic practitioners help countless clients move through several of the four levels of healing especially on the mythic and energetic levels. When it comes down to changing the physical and mental levels, that's when one takes one's own responsibility to sign up for change and ultimately transformation. There is at least one element where nobody can have a hold over you and that is the element of the mind. That's where most changes happen, whether it's changing one's perspective or deciding to change elements of one's lifestyle. The mind (your own microcosm) has the innate and phenomenal ability to change anything!

The Seed of Our Becoming

In life we start our Earth's journey as a seed, one that is gestated over many months in the safety of the womb. We are cared for and kept out of harm's way. We come into this world with the possibility of our sacred journey, and as the soul keeps the details of that purpose safe, we live the life our path dictates. Now there can be confusion along the way, as many factors filter into our beings, whether it's the influence of our parents, schools, religions, friends and peers, or circumstance. This is when the seed is at its most vulnerable; when it's under the influences of the belief systems foisted on us, or learned from any of the above. How this happens, and if we survive, is mainly down to circumstance.

The Seed Germinates
Old Belief Systems and Generational Patterns

Who and what your ancestors believed in plays a part in who you are today, just the same as you and your partner's DNA plays a part in your children's fundamental nature. Just like a cocktail that is concocted with many differing components, we carry within us a cocktail of genes and DNA. This cocktail creates the way we act and conduct ourselves; all fuelled in some way by the belief systems of our ancestors.

Let me talk a little of my own grandparents' lives...

They were both born into the working classes at the end of the 19th Century. Neither of them came from a privileged background. I never really knew what ethics they had towards money other than what my own mother had told me. I do know that they readily accepted their place in society, working within the class structure that was more palpable back then. My grandparents' belief systems were based around hard work, and working and saving for what they needed. I guess I was too young to understand their true ethics. All I knew was that if money wasn't there, it wasn't there. They also lived through two World Wars, with rationing and coupons.

How does/did this influence my own belief systems?

Well, money matters play a part in all of our lives in differing ways. There are two ways to look at it. If the belief system of my grandparents was that money should be earned and saved so that you have the money to buy what you need, then this would influence how my mother and I view money. On the one hand it becomes something to save for a rainy day, which in itself is stagnant and on the other hand, it becomes something else to squander and spend. This is like a double bind, due to the influences of war-time rationing.

There is an opposite belief system of needing abundance, as the war's influence ensured that there was never enough to go round. This can be seen time after time during the post-war years. There are generations who still hoard tins of food in case of a lean time. I always remember my mother-in-law's cupboards being crammed with tinned goods and her freezer crammed to bursting with frozen meat.

But how does all this influence who we are now?

By taking a step back in time, looking at your own ancestors' lives (mother father, grandparents, uncles, aunts, etc.) consider some facts about their lives...

What type of society did they grow up in? How did they live? What jobs did they do? What events were prominent in their lives (if any)? What belief systems influenced them? Examine their health issues. Look at your ancestors' history by either examining their illnesses or how they died. Ask yourselves whether it was to due to heart problems, tuberculosis, cancer, respiratory problems, overweight issues, cholera or starvation. Are there any signs of these illnesses in current family members?

Maybe go a bit deeper, thinking outside the box: Are there any recurring events or issues that seem to be replaying themselves throughout the generations of your family?

Are there issues that may include a type of 'family curse'; family members who are dying at a certain age; or members who encounter a similar type of accident, illness or misfortune?

A Personal Example – My Husband's Ancestral Curse

Let me share with you a personal story. We only discovered this 'family curse' during recent research into my husband's family genealogy. It was whilst delving into Paul's family tree, looking at marriage and death certificates, that we unearthed a definitive repeat pattern that astounded us both!

Within my husband's family dynamics, there appeared to be a type of curse or repeat pattern that befell the men folk around the ages of 42. This curse was traced as far back as the late 1800s, around 1898. This was as far back as we could go.

When we attempted to find out which family members were affected, we could only establish it as far back to my husband's great, great grandfather (James). James owned a successful printing company in London. The story starts on one particular Christmas Eve when James' business and many others in the vicinity literally went up in smoke... completely destroyed by fire! The result of this fire left James desolate. Sadly, he was not insured. Consequently, shortly after the fire, James fell into financial difficulties and, by the age of 42, the stress and worry of it all finally killed him.

He was survived by his wife Elizabeth and seven children, aged between three and 17 years old. Very soon after James' death Elizabeth also died! Whether from a broken heart or the fear of being left alone, penniless and having to bring up her seven children, we shall never really know.

The seven children became orphans due to the lack of close family members that could afford to take them in. Many, sadly, ended up in orphanages.

Two of them, due to their ages, went into military service. My husband's grandfather was one of the orphans. His name was Frances. He stayed in London, and eventually married and had his own children. He also had his own business, a hardware shop.

Here is where the 'curse' seemed to replay itself! He too, in his early 40s, had an accident and fell from a ladder. This caused him to be bed-ridden; a consequence that resulted in him being unable to continue with his business. He saw out the rest of his days in pain and poverty.

Following on from this, one of his sons, Laurence (my husband's father), aged 18, took up a career in the Army. Just before he went into service he married Eva (Paul's mum) and soon after went off to war, returning home some three years later. Eva and Lawrence had three children together. Many years later, completely out of the blue, Laurence decided that the family would emigrate to South Africa as part of the '£10 incentive initiative' of the time, designed to bring much-needed skilled labour into their country.

Laurence was a skilled engineer. So, off they all went to start a new life in South Africa that would provide them all with an escape from England and hopefully, a better lifestyle. After one problem then another, Eva decided that she wanted to go back home. She felt she needed to be with her daughter who had stayed in the UK and was expecting her first child.

So, off she went, leaving behind the two boys; (Paul) my husband and (Barry) his brother. Life went on until one day Paul arrived home, only to find his father had gone. Paul was left in an empty house... all alone!

In time, he was eventually taken in and cared for by a South African family. He only saw his father once more after that. Here is where the story and 'curse' seemed to re-appear.

Laurence was in his early 40s during this time.

Whatever it was that drove him away we shall never know, but we found out that he had died in Cape Town, aged 46.

Let me now bring you forward in this story to the middle of the 1990s.

My husband, also now in his early 40s, had a complete emotional breakdown! This came as a great shock to us. We assumed this was due to a past unhappy history that was seemingly rearing its ugly head again. After some soul-searching he felt it necessary to revisit the time when he had been left alone in South Africa.

We believe these emotions he was experiencing were sparked off when our eldest daughter, who was aged eight or nine at the time, reminded him of how vulnerable a child is at that age. It had brought back many bad memories to Paul and raising the question: How could anyone ever contemplate leaving a child of that age alone?

Paul's breakdown sent him on a voyage of discovery; the darkness and healing eventually ending up as a complete life change. Not only that, but he felt a profound need to heal the family line by removing the pattern or curse that had claimed many of the menfolk in his family.

However, many of us account for similar events like illnesses, accidents, behavioural obsessions, alcoholism, addictions, bad luck and even the lack of love. Many continually replay themselves in subsequent generations over and over again, until the pattern is healed.

Germinating Behaviours

The way we behave has much to do with some of the difficulties that we face today. Our responses, the way we communicate with others, how we are and act within a given situation, are all down to our character (our own personal life script).

How does our character inform us?

Character is learnt; whether it has been developed by life's experiences or from our parents' beliefs. Our character, the current essence of who we are, can explain many things. It can explain *how* and *why* we interact in certain ways with others; how our relationships are formed; and maybe even the reasons why we may have such strong views about things. I remember, as part of my own story, how some of the events I had experienced were responsible for creating part of *my* own character.

I had learned to generate my own nature in order to keep myself emotionally safe.

Now that was *not* something I was born with. Consequently, when it has been generated by yourself, it becomes a behavioural nature; one that can be hard to change.

Whether the behavioural pattern comes from our genes or we have self-evolved it, it is an important aspect of who and what we are and it should be recognised.

These patterns can be held deep within our subconscious as shadow aspects; those that remain hidden and buried until something *triggers* them. Then, when the blue touch paper is ignited... watch out!

I remember being taught during my training with the Four Winds Society, that there is a Racist, Sexist, Hitler and George W Bush in all of us; just waiting for the chance to be brought out into the open, even though many of us become adept at hiding them. The problem with hiding these aspects is that we are often in denial of their existence, not realising that they are a part of us...

One lazy afternoon we were all sat in class in Dunderry Park. Our teacher was asking us to tell her about a person that we intensely disliked! One particular American lady spoke viciously about her hatred for George Bush:

'I really hate George Bush!' she retorted. 'Really,' our teacher (who was also from the U.S.) replied, 'Why is that?'

'Well,' the student replied, 'He is a bully, is arrogant, and barges his way into places he shouldn't!'

'Okay,' our teacher replied, 'Let me ask you this. When was the last time you behaved bullish and barged into something you shouldn't have?'

The American lady went very red; she sat and thought about the question, almost stuttering her reply; she then went on to recount the many times that she had acted in exactly the same way as she had described that George Bush had... only towards other people in her life!

Our teacher simply smiled a 'knowing smile' and led us towards illuminating our shadows.

The Path Towards Illumination and Awareness

This is it, the crux of the abyss; now what do you do? Do you carry on reading this book and put it away, never to be seen again, adopting the role of conscious stagnation or do you do something radical and life changing? Do you sign up to cease the role of wounded victim? Do you exercise that most precious of gifts, free will and say to yourself, 'If I change nothing then nothing changes'? And if you decide to adopt the latter statement, then I say to you; 'Why not start the change today?'

Those life experiences which have placed us where we are today shouldn't be seen as negative. Should we allow the influence of those experiences to become our script, a script which, like the most tragic of plays, holds us within the grip of misery, whereby we convince ourselves that we deserve the misery our lives have afforded us (and because of that we certainly do not deserve to be whole and happy again)?

There is a mythic story called Ariadne's Golden Thread which illustrates the way that old folk stories and fairy tales have the ability to show us how we can pull ourselves out of any preverbal hole by showing us how our experiences in life are not necessarily finite. On the contrary the wisdom of the myth serves as a lantern which can illuminate our dark days showing us the way to freedom.

Princess Ariadne, daughter of King Minos of Crete, helped Theseus slay her monstrous half-brother, known as the Minotaur, by teaching him to use a golden thread as a path within the labyrinth where the Minotaur lived. Deep within that dark maze where no man or woman had ever survived the Minotaur's savagery, Theseus killed the monster, and then followed the gold thread to freedom. When he emerged triumphant from the labyrinth, Theseus claimed Ariadne for his own. As they sailed the world, Ariadne was certain she had won the heart of the hero in return for her brilliance, her loyalty, and her love. After all, she had betrayed those closest to her to save Theseus.

When Theseus finally brought their ship to the faraway island of Naxos, Ariadne thought they would live there forever in bliss. Instead, he abandoned her on the island, sailing off without an apology. Such was her thanks for saving him. Alone, Ariadne forgot her triumph as the untangler of the labyrinth. She was Ariadne the forsaken, Ariadne the foolish, rather than Ariadne the beloved of Theseus.

At first, the heartbroken princess wept. Then she thought of killing herself out of shame and sorrow. But the Muses took pity upon Ariadne. They hovered around the poor girl as soft as winds, and whispered into her ear of a worthier love and a loftier fate. This made no sense to the girl for she could not see beyond her abandonment by Theseus. But soon Ariadne saw a bronze chariot appear on the horizon. The Muses whispered it held a new bridegroom for Ariadne, the man she was fated to love. As the chariot drew closer, Ariadne saw it was draped in vines and clusters of ripe grapes—for this chariot was driven by Dionysus, god of divine intoxication, who loved Ariadne for her passionate bravery and loyalty. Ariadne's heart was immediately healed by Dionysus's admiration and loving embrace. She soon forgot about Theseus and accepted her happy fate. Dionysus and Ariadne were wed. Made a goddess by love, Ariadne lived forever with her immortal husband in ecstatic triumph.

The Labyrinth symbolises the confusing experiences of our Earth walk. The Minotaur represents the dangers that could harm us, the golden thread represents the lantern of wisdom which shows us the way out, and the muses reflect that soft spiritual voice of our soul as it gently guides us back from the dark.

The Lantern Illuminates

Tennyson's poem Ulysses can be thought to symbolise embarking on a path of healing as a way of dreaming a new world into being. As the aged Ulysses stood on the deck of his ship in readiness to begin another new adventure, he asked his shipmates to strike the oars as he told them that 'it's not too late to seek a newer world'.

It is *never* too late, you are never too old, too wounded or too sad, especially when we realise that we are both captain and navigator of our own ship through life, as we mythically raise our sails and begin the journey towards the Island of Harmony.

Chapter 13

Physical and Mental Illness in Modern Society

We live in a fear-driven society where our health is one of the only things that may interfere with this wonderful material life we have forged for ourselves. The Western medical system is bursting at the seams as it tries to cope with large numbers of patients who make appointments daily, and those who require surgery, let alone the onslaught of emotional problems that doctors are faced with. The medical system decries some alternative health therapies, Shamanism being one. Why? Because it cannot scientifically measure a Shamanic process or the benefits it offers. Scientists look at Shamanic healing as either voodoo or having a placebo effect. Shamans would answer that by saying... it doesn't matter! Because we believe if we can make ourselves ill, then we can damn well make ourselves better again!

We are well versed in Western society to go running to the doctor as soon as anything inwardly threatens our health. Whether it's a virus that swamps our body or a pain that won't go away, we are grateful to have an organisation where we can go and get it checked out. We know that the doctor will either give us a prescription for some drugs, which may or may not cure the illness, or we will be sent to the hospital for further tests.

The downside of this system is that we rely on the doctor analysing our symptoms and effectively administrating the correct drug, in less than 15 minutes of consultation time. The doctor will see the patient over many visits; it's a bit like a trial and error type of scenario in order to fully determine the cause of the symptoms, offering many different combinations of drugs in the process. When many avenues are exhausted the patient may be referred to a psychotherapist or for counselling, though by the time the patient finally gets an appointment, it could be months and months down the line, depending on each country's mandate and resources.

Now there is nothing wrong with the medical profession per se, but we are somewhat reliant on a system which subscribes to the fact that symptom + prescription = cure. In many cases that equation is adequate, but personally I think that in possibly around 60% of medical cases, a pharmaceutical drug will only serve to either suppress, or delay, the necessary patient care.

By now, we understand that pharmaceutical drugs cannot be a generic cure for all. Though human bodies contain the same components as each other, that's probably where the similarities end. Why a drug doesn't have the same result on patients exhibiting the same symptoms is a far bigger minefield. That's possibly because how each one of us copes with either illness or emotional upset is different. When it comes to emotionally fed illnesses, other than psychology, there isn't too much a doctor can do to help. Even a psychologist can only be of assistance on the mental level; they do not intercede at the level of the emotional wounding, as that requires skilled intervention on the energetic and mythical planes to remove the affinity we hold to the initial wound (I will go into that in more detail in the next chapter).

What is now absent from the current medical system is the ability to be able to talk about our problems in detail whether they are related to an illness or not, as its only by discussing where we have come from and what we have experienced can we then fully prescribe what a patient needs. Anyone who has had a problem and has been able to talk it out with a non-biased individual will know just how good that feels. When a client arrives at a Shamanic consultation they have the whole stage, and are able to narrate their life-story without any judgement or criticism. Sometimes it's such a blessed relief to be able to release the energy connected to the words related to a wounding!

A Shaman knows that any physical or mental illness is related to how ill at ease a client's spirit is. Hence, the word disease: if you break it down it means dis...ease. Any disharmony with one's own spirit can cause all manner of maladies.

Case Study: Sexual Abuse

James goes to the doctor feeling really anxious; his whole body aches. He suffers from symptoms of nausea and palpitations. There is a voice chattering away in his head constantly. The doctor checks his blood pressure and listens to his heart, and asks James what other symptoms he is experiencing. James relays the best he can by trying to describe how his body feels, and from the information given, the doctor prescribes some calming medication usually in the form of an anti-depressant. James goes home, takes the anti-depressant and feels calmer, but his head is still racing and his whole body still feels ill at ease.

James comes to see a Shaman; he is given plenty of time to tell the Shaman how he feels physically, but then the Shaman asks him about the health of his mother, father and other family members. He is also asked about his life as a child and subsequently how his life has served him up to the present day. During the consultation James will tell the Shaman that he was repeatedly abused as a child, by both his father and uncle. The Shaman then asks James to lie down on the plinth and will test his energy usually via the chakras, possibly determining that the base chakra is not functioning. The Shaman provides a clearing. During the clearing James's body is writhing and twitching as the Shaman releases the energy connected to the memories of the abuse. After the session James feels relaxed and has a sense of peace that he has never felt before. James will come back and see the Shaman for a further four or so visits, each time releasing heavy energy connected to the abuse wound at a deeper level each time. James even has the chance to dialogue with the abusers on an energetic level, in the safe environment of a sacred healing space, which allows James the ability to benefit from a sense of justice. He also gains a deeper understanding of his wound. The sessions leave James free as each time he regains a part of his self back again.

Case Study: Cancer

Molly is a woman in her 60s and has been diagnosed with cancer. She is already a seeker on a spiritual path, and she is determined not to subscribe to the current western modality of cancer treatment. She elects to discover the benefits of cleansing the body by methods involving deep detox as well as boosting her now wholesome diet with specific and beneficial supplements, among many other things.

Cancer, like other physical ailments also has an emotional source. Molly comes along to see a Shaman for an intensive healing experience. During the consultation Molly relays the script of her life; her relationships with men, getting married, having children, and how her adult life has served her. The Shaman starts the initial cleansing of any heavy energy related to the wounds Molly talks about.

As each consultation begins Molly remembers more information. From the displacement her Jewish culture endured, to the fact that her own Mother died of cancer, in her 60s, as well as her younger sister who passed away with cancer in her 50s, now the Shaman is dealing with a repeat pattern of cancer. It affected the female members in Molly's family. The Shaman now works to break the pattern by means of Shamanic processes. The intensive healing ends with talking to Molly about her life in the future; suggesting tools for Molly to use as well as further consultations if Molly needs them.

Molly told me she experienced the healing as undeniable proof that she had the means to heal herself, with the help and guidance of the shaman. The experience also strengthened her intuitive understanding that the illness was actually a great gift sent to accelerate her healing at a much deeper level and to open up new worlds about whose existence she had had no previous knowledge.

Case Study: The Unborn Twin

Jane's case is really unusual and one that I haven't seen before. Although as a Shaman, I feel it is possible that it will certainly not be an isolated case.

Jane is in her mid-40s and came to see me as she suffered with bouts of extreme low energy; she also had a physical condition of fibromyalgia and problems with her digestion. Doctors tested Jane for rheumatoid arthritis, the results came back negative.

I had been working with Jane for several months and for about a week or two after her sessions she would feel great, her energy would return and she enjoyed life. But following that, a repeat pattern re-emerged and Jane would experience similar symptoms of energy loss again. It was really becoming quite a puzzle, so I suggested to her that she visit a Soul Reader.

(*A soul reading involves a sacred meeting between you and your Higher Self. It is an opportunity for you to come face to face with your soul essence, a place where you can access a map of your full potential in the areas of health, wealth, relationships and life purpose. It allows that newly-found knowledge, or deep remembering, to guide you forward on your path*).

The findings were both incredible and amazing! What had happened to Jane, happened long ago, way back in her mother's womb. Jane was originally a twin... although her twin never survived; and her mother may not have known at the time that she was even carrying twins.

Even though the physical body of the twin didn't make it, its energy body certainly did... and it lived on long and virulent in Jane's body. The reading uncovered that the twin was a boy and his age was around eight or nine years oldn human years; and this boy was literally playing havoc inside Jane's body. When she was active, he slept; when he was active, Jane was exhausted.

The session Jane and I had following this reading, was quite literally astounding! When Jane arrived, she showed me her stomach; both Jane and I were astonished to see that it was both pregnant-like and solid in its outward appearance. As Jane lay on the plinth, I started work; I knew that I had to perform the Death Rites on Jane's deceased mother as well as the unborn twin (this process ensures that the soul leaves the physical body free of any wounds that are left unhealed).

Her mother's part went without a hitch, but performing death rites on an energy soul, and quite a precocious soul at that, left me with a difficult job, a task, however, I need not have worried about.

As all of a sudden, an elderly Qero woman appeared holding a birthing blanket in her hands! She telepathically told me to hold Jane's stomach to encourage the soul towards the birth channel... she then swiftly and expertly birthed the unborn twin through Jane's birthing canal. She placed him on Jane's stomach and I was then able to perform the death rites on him; I even had a tear in my eye as he left skipping hand-in-hand with his mother towards the light.

As I was closing the healing session, I suddenly felt a greyish energy moving around Jane's body. I knew that this energy should not stay. In a flash, a portal opened up above me and an angel-like being swooped down and whisked the energy off in its arms, the portal closed behind... All of this leaving me with mouth agape!

After the session, Jane's stomach had returned to normal and she felt great. As you can imagine, she was extremely relieved and literally skipped out of the treatment room.

I wanted to give you a flavour of the types of situations and wounds a Shaman has to deal with. In the next chapter I go into the alchemical process of healing in greater detail.

Chapter 14

The Alchemical Process of Healing

If you came to see a Shaman and he/she gave you a pill to make it all better, wouldn't you feel more at ease? When I undertake a first consultation with a client one of the things I ask them is: 'If I waved my magic wand, what would improve your current situation?' Asking this question sometimes results in a tearful release, as the mere thought of someone actually asking and offering to help you to feel better without any chemicals is sometimes hard to even imagine.

Undertaking a Shamanic process of healing isn't always easy, but it *is* effective. Within many indigenous cultures the young men would set out on a challenge or quest (usually one that would test both their courage and spirituality) as a way of a marking a turning point in life. These quests were often embarked on before puberty with the intention of finding themselves in order to become a man, and earn their right to sit alongside their peers. In Shamanic cultures, especially those within the Native merican tribes, they would often create a medicine wheel or sacred hoop for use in both healing and for teaching purposes. In South America one would create a healing Mesa.

For anyone to embark on a Shamanic healing journey a medicine wheel provides a perfect model, whereby one can feel they are embarking on a healing quest. This is marked and celebrated as each direction is worked.

(A medicine wheel, whether its origins are from Native America, or another part of the world, is usually sectioned off into the four directions: North, West, South and East).

The Medicine Wheel as a Healing Process

A healing process is commenced upon as a journey to heal our wounds by exploring the self by way of self-realisation. Only when we know ourselves completely in full colour, warts and all, can we finally understand why our Earth-walk has been a challenging one, and why it is we have attracted certain people and events into our lives.

To fully appreciate a Shamanic healing modality, it is best illustrated by interweaving some of my own journey in training and healing, using the Peruvian Qero teachings, as taught by The Four Winds Society. As I said earlier we follow the four directions; in the South Americas the start point is in the South...

The South... Serpent Sheds her Skin

One fine November day in 2002, Paul and I naively headed off into our first class. We were both feeling nervous and unsure of what was about to happen. Sure enough, we fell facedown on the 'path of serpent'. (Serpent is one of the four archetypes encountered on the South American medicine wheel. Each archetype, in its own right, accompanies you while you process each direction. It does this by lending the archetypal essence of each of the animals' natures).

Serpent requests, or should I say insists, that we shed those negative life experiences which have formed our lives; the abuse we suffered as children or the bullying that occurred in junior school, even the rape that happened when we were 12 years old. Whatever the wound, and how much importance we have placed around the story connected to the event, it needs to be released and shed.

For those of you who do not already know: serpent does not shed its skin easily! On the contrary, it goes to great lengths to shed it... it writhes and twists; using all of its energy until it finally breaks free of its old, outgrown skin. It is during this process that the snake is at its most vulnerable. Just like snake, we too need to become vulnerable; *trusting* that the shedding will ensure continued growth and wellbeing. This is *exactly* what we need to do in order for us to be released from our wounds and issues; emerging free of the entanglements of our pasts.

The first day of the South direction had started...
   Somewhat nervously, we experienced our very first fire ceremony. We were both getting used to being in such a large community of 'nubile Shamans'; a group who would go on to relate such intimate details of their lives; openly cry; rant; and eat and drink together. In the following months/years we would become a large bonded community.
   We were both feeling a little fearful of what was to come...
   We all sat down, mainly on the floor, with brand new notebooks and pens poised to write down the wisdom teachings that we were about to hear. After a beautiful and enlightening talk given by Alberto Villoldo, we took part in our very first personal healing exercise...
   Each of us had brought with us three stones. These were to be the beginning of the building of our own personal healing bundles (called Mesas).
   Firstly, we needed to programme them by shedding our wounds and issues. (A Shaman will use stones and crystals as part of his or her mesa as they are from the Earth and have endured aeons of transformation. They become very powerful aides for personal healing and growth. Stones and crystals connect the Shaman to the Earth energies, protecting as well as having the ability to absorb negative energy, transforming it into light. A Shaman's mesa usually contains 13 stones - three for each direction plus one gifted from your teacher and the lineage).
   I think it is fair to say that we started the exercise feeling timid, clumsy and with confused emotions. We all paired off and started to experience what it felt like to let go of some of our personal issues.
   My turn eventually came to play the part of Shaman; my partner played the role of client. I assumed the learned position and watched with mouth agape as her body quivered and convulsed, all quite uncon-

trollably. Briefly, I allowed my ego mind to convince me that surely she was putting all this on!

I was concentrating so hard to apply the correct process; with my eyes shut, I became aware of the sounds that filled the room; they were ungodly and animal like!

All of a sudden I cautiously opened one eye and I turned my head to make sure that we weren't being invaded by marauding jungle animals or monsters!

I watched in utter astonishment as other clients, who were going through the same convulsive and quivering motions, were letting go and releasing past traumatic experiences. It was at that very moment that I realised that we had embarked on something very magical, powerful and spiritual. My mind was racing to try to make sense of what I was seeing, desperately trying to put this scene into a place where I could accept that what I was seeing was normal! How foolish was I?

The fact of the matter was that I was part of a room filled by 60 or 70 individuals gathered together in this beautiful mansion; obviously like-minded people, although from many varying backgrounds; all with one aim in mind… We all wanted to heal ourselves from life's wounds and experiences, and be able to do the same for others.

We all wanted to 'walk a new path and find answers', one that would be both fantastical and challenging.

Very soon it was my turn to unburden my wounds; my ego mind informing me that I certainly would not be convulsing and quivering, that's for sure. As the process began, I too went with the overwhelming emotion that oozed from me, and sure enough I found myself devoid of any urging, convulsing and squirming. Instead I felt my body instinctually pulse as it released itself of several years of wounds. After the process had subsided, I remember leaving the classroom for the day feeling quite shell-shocked and numb, wondering what else the following days might have in store for us.

The West

It was April 2003; five months had passed since our first course. We had returned to continue our training as 'Western Shamans'...

Most of us had been through a most exhausting and testing time, and I do not say that glibly. We had all experienced the effects of shedding our past; arriving already exhausted and thinking to ourselves; 'Surely the West direction cannot be as bad as the South class was? Surely we had finished the pain of personal healing? Hadn't we?' How wrong could we have been!

We spent some time sitting in circle and catching up with our classmates. The 'talking stick' was passed around as we listened in astonishment and with empathy as our fellow students relayed their stories and experiences of the last five months. And then, without any word of warning it began... the 'Way of Jaguar'... the path of the West.

Well, here we were. We had arrived at a place where we had to learn how to step beyond our fears to become the luminous warrior who has no enemies in this world or the next. We learned to practice peace by becoming peace. It was time once again to let go of our old stories and old belief systems. We were shown how our heritage and family lines sap our energy.

We had to discover the things that drained our energy; draining it so much that it could stop us from following our destiny. We discovered that we could inherit illnesses and curses from other people, including from our own ancestral lineage. We entered into the world of 'our shadow', those aspects of the self that we had disowned.

We were taught to understand how we lock away so much of our energy by *disowning* our shadow selves; how we should uncover and acknowledge these shadows, and how *not* to project them on to others.

We learnt how death 'stalks us like a jungle cat stalks her prey'!

We learnt how humans fear death; how we should celebrate death, not as an end, but as a beginning. Death was inevitable and an event that we had experienced many times before.

We learnt how we as humans manage our problems, over-analysing them to desperately find a solution. We began to understand why we only seek solutions using our ego mind.

We were taught how to remove energies that had lodged themselves within our energy bodies; heavy energy that had become crystallised or fluid. These are intrusive and can be linked to either a loved one that has passed; or from a person who had held rage or anger towards us. (We can even create a dark living energy ourselves, one that becomes both elemental and chaotic, fed by destructive thoughts of anger, frustration or unhappiness).

What an intensive week it turned out to be.

We were split into groups of six. Each group had to practise conducting a fluid extraction as well as having one removed from ourselves.

As the session went on it was nearing the time when I too had to experience having an entity removed!

Before the process I began to feel very grumpy and withdrawn (this is quite unlike me). Before my turn arrived we had had a tea break. Off I went for my green tea and I didn't even dip into the biscuit tin (again very unusual). The group went outside to get some fresh air. Normally this was a time of relief and laughter; a time spent chatting on the steps and swapping stories. This time, however, I felt really unsociable. I could hardly bring myself to chat with others. Even when a friend asked if I was okay, I replied: 'No I'm not! I have the hump and I do not want to do this exercise.'

Too soon the break was over. Slowly we traipsed back into the hall. I actually said to my group that I felt like something inside of me was taking over as if it was trying to avoid being tampered with.

The feeling I was experiencing was really odd. It was like my whole being was trying to escape this exercise. My ego mind was desperately trying to scheme how I could avoid this extraction; every sense I possessed left me, I had never felt anything like this before. Reluctantly, as I knew we all had to participate, the process began.

Someone stood behind me, running energy up my spine. Two others stood either side at my shoulders, tracking where the energy was moving. I felt scared and claustrophobic...

The Shaman, who held a crystal in her hand, took hold of my hand. She was waiting for the energy to move from its hiding place in my body, down my arm, so that she could then trap it inside the crystal and remove it.

I felt very detached from what was going on around me. Inside I felt a rampant energy that was swelling up inside my stomach, moving upwards through my solar plexus. When this energy arrived at my heart area, I felt sick and weak; I had a feeling of anger raging inside. I could not place this anger for some time, but eventually I began to recognise what it was.

The Shaman moved the energy towards my shoulder and down my arm. At this point I felt its intensity weakening as she finally removed it via my hand and safely into the crystal. I could have collapsed as it left; I was rocking back and forth and was told to sit down and relax. After drinking a little water, I explained to my group what I felt it was...

Some six months earlier, I had worked with a young man who was a university graduate. He had taken on a job that was very much beneath his capability. After a short period of time it became apparent that he was a very unsettled young man; one who kept everything to himself. You could detect his underlying unhappiness by his demeanour.

After several disagreements over one thing or another, it became clear that the two of us would never see eye to eye. He became withdrawn and began making mistakes. Very soon it became obvious that he really disliked me. It soon progressed to a point where he had to be removed from our office. I knew he blamed me for that... and he finally left.

I recognised the entity that had been removed as the anger and rage that he had been directing towards me over a time. This was never verbally, but rather a toxic energy that he had directed at me… simply by the power of emotion and feeling alone.

After the energy had been removed, a lightness and freedom took over my body. I could not believe how good I felt. I could have skipped naked around the grounds of Dunderry.

The real concern is that one hardly ever realises that one has become a victim of an'intrusive energy, one that has been directed towards you using the power of hatred, anger, dislike or fear. Although it is a little difficult to describe, there is a distinct sense of disharmony taking place inside of you; a sense that you really do not feel well in the sense of spritely or positive. You do sense, however, that there is an unnameable and invisible feeling of heaviness inside you. Unfortunately, it is a feeling that is being fed by another's unhappiness and dislike and is directed towards you.

Once again, we left Ireland and returned to England; both in a complete daze, but knowing that something had been shifted and healed. The following five months went by without too much hassle or angst. Weeks and months passed and it was soon time to return to our now beloved Dunderry Park.

The North

It was mid-October. With much excitement inside our bellies we looked forward to the 'epic journey of Hummingbird'… the path of the North; the place of our Ancestors.

Hummingbird symbolises strength, ability and endurance. These tiny little birds, some no larger than your thumb, can travel up to 3,000 miles. Archetypically, they signify the epic journey that we undertake in life, reminding us to 'drink directly from the nectar of life', and more importantly, they remind us to experience joy.

I loved this direction and its teachings; it felt comfortable being in a place of remembering. Its teachings included a journey into the mystery; a place where we practise infinity. The class was also taught how to master time, enabling us to break free from the grip of the Western idea of time constraints.

Breaking free from the grip of time – what a task, when *everything* we do is usually governed by the clock.

Tick tock, time to get up... tick tock, must rush to work... tick tock, time for lunch... tick tock, what a relief home-time... tick, tock, must pick the kids up...tick tock, must cook dinner...tick tock, must get the kids to bed... tick tock, I must exercise... tick tock, must go to bed...

The clock dictates our lives and everything we do! We are programmed with time restraints and time slots, trapped within those 24-hour intervals. We also learned how to become invisible by not leaving imprints of where we had trodden.

Thinking globally: how much evidence is left behind indicating where humans have been? Tell-tale signs like rubbish, pollution, packaging and destruction.

The North is where we relinquished our roles and our belief in the characters we believed that we were (as described earlier in the book).

We understood how we could become confined and defined by the roles we adopt.

Best of all, we were taught soul retrieval, a process that is taken on by a Shaman on behalf of a client, to retrieve a soul part that has become fragmented. Soul loss indicates a loss of safety. It usually occurs following a trauma such as rape, abuse or even abortion.

We were delighted to be trained by Alberto Villoldo himself for this section.

He taught us how to travel to the lower world; a place where we track the line of our ancestors. Then we would travel to the middle world, a place that signifies current time, mirroring the level that we are on now. Finally, we travelled to the upper world where we can track our destinies.

We even went further upwards to discover a further five domains of the upper world. Here we visited the realm of the stone people; the realm of the plant people; the realm of the animal spirits; upwards to the realm of our ancestors; finally to the highest level… the realm of who we shall become, what an incredible journey.

We were also taught how to process problems through our mesa (medicine bundle). We were taught to take the problem *away* from the literal into the energetic, so that we could no longer collude with it. This is such a great lesson and the very reason that I suggest you create sand paintings and carry out fire ceremonies.

Humans do love to engage their egos in problem solving. I am *not* talking about working out who is going to pick the kids up from school, etc. I am talking about the types of problems that we allow to fill our minds, those that we allow to become heady.

We use ego as an analytical tool, only resulting in all of our energy becoming captive in solving the problem. By doing this, we cannot seem to find any release or resolution to that problem until we finally have an answer.

We were practising and carrying out soul retrievals; this time we were practising a different type of soul retrieval. We were looking for something that wraps itself around the soul and holds the soul in a vice-like grip.

We split off into pairs and this time around I was paired with Paul. He got himself comfortable on the floor and I began…

I was using my rattle to enable me to journey downwards to the realm of the underworld – the place of our ancestors. I remember allowing my luminous body to head down through the earth; cleansing it in the underground rivers and streams as it was carried along to its destination.

Eventually I arrived at a grassy embankment and was met by my two power animals: Deer and Owl. They accompany me whilst journeying to warn me of any impending danger. They also go ahead into places that I do not venture into until I feel it is safe to do so.

I walked up the grassy embankment where I was met by the Keeper of the Underworld. I asked his permission to enter and gave him my reasons for being there. He swung the gate open and allowed me to pass.

As I entered the first area I was met by a burning building, an inferno. Rafters were falling all around me. I felt danger! As I turned around I saw a gentleman who I knew to be my husband's great grandfather, James Kenyon. He stood there totally distraught as he watched the building going up in smoke.

I went over to him and asked him why he just stood there watching the fire consume his business. He turned around, with a forlorn look of desperation and said: 'It is just no good trying to be successful in this life!'

At this point, I immediately knew that he was making a Contract, one that would turn out to not only be his undoing, but the undoing of many generations to come.

I continued to rattle in a clockwise motion over Paul's heart chakra. I opened the chakra and used a crystal to unwind and remove the tendrils of that Contract. I did this to ensure that it would stop informing Paul in the way of a generational curse.

As I was removing the long, thick, tight and blackened tendrils, I spoke to James again. I discussed with him the seriousness of the words that he had used and how those words would possibly affect every generation that followed him.

He slowly began to understand, and he changed those damning words to a new contract: 'Life is to be lived and experienced'.

As he said those words out aloud, I watched his face change. The forlorn look of desperation had left him; he smiled, waved and then headed off towards the light. As he left, he gave me a gift of a book. I blew this gift into Paul's heart chakra, along with the new contract.

If you remember the story about generational curses back in the

*Chapter The Alchemical Process of Transformation, you will see how
the contract that was initially made by James, 'It is no good trying to be
successful in this life', very much affected the generations that followed
him... including Paul!*

*The importance of changing those damning words was imperative,
not only for the generations that went before, but also for Paul and our
daughters and our daughters' children.*

*Even more amazing is how James' contract was wrapping itself
around Paul's soul, holding it deep in the underworld, engaged in those
very damning words! Paul may possibly have never become free of it
unless he had received that Underworld Soul Extraction.*

After yet another wonderful and amazing week, we left our now
very dear friends and headed back to England, once again armed
with many tools to help strengthen us.

For further in-depth information on Journeying and Soul
Retrieval, may I suggest that you read: *Soul Retrieval, Retrieving
the Fragmented Self* by Sandra Ingerman and *Mending the Past,
Healing the Future* by Dr Alberto Villoldo.

Another five months passed and it was now March 2004. This
time the trip was slightly tinged with sadness as we knew it
would possibly be the last time that these 60/70 people would
actually be together in the same space. We knew that we would
have to say farewell to so many friends from all over the world.

Come Fly with Me to the East

This time there weren't awkward silences as we approached
Dunderry; instead there were just whoops and squeals of utter
delight as we once again greeted our friends.

There were high spirits and giggling as we congregated on the
steps of the house, all enjoying the beautiful spring sunshine.
Even when our teacher 'rattled us' into class, we almost skipped
in; this time without fear or trepidation.

However, our teacher uttered the following words: 'They say

the work of the East is all light and airy... but beware, there *will* be turbulence!'

'Oh great,' we all thought, 'how can anything be as disturbing as the 'Shedding of the South' and the 'Shadows of the West'?'

Well, I jest with you not... *DISTURBING IT WAS!*

We were beginning our journey with Eagle/Condor, birds that are greatly revered by the Qero – the very same birds that fly high above the earth, seeing all from a much wider perspective; flying wing to wing with Great Spirit. We had stepped onto the pathway of the East.

Many of us believed that when we arrived in the East that our journey towards personal growth was ending. In fact, it had just started. Here we learned that *everything* is sacred and that reality is just a myth that we have not quite seen through yet.

We dabbled with the possibility of 'throwing everything out there', allowing spirit to take control of our destiny.

We learnt how to move everything in our lives around, without knowing the outcome, by performing a 'Huaca' (where one can create a ripple in space and time). Here we dip into the infinite and raw energy of spirit, where there is *no* measured outcome; a terrifying thought and a terrifying process.

This process seemed to de-stabilise most of the class. We strongly questioned our teacher as to its validity and the wisdom of performing it.

During this class we were taught the 'Great Death Rites'. The Death Rites are a wonderful and beautiful process that can be given to a person as they prepare to leave this Earth.

The Death Rites allow a dying person the chance to recapitulate his or her life by telling stories that may have wounds or regrets attached to them. This special time is a chance to heal those wounds and regrets by clearing away any toxic energy to enable the soul to journey home *free* of this life's wounds, freeing the soul so that it may evolve *without* having to come back in another lifetime to put things right.

The story of Eva's journey home

My mother-in-law, the infamous Eva, had become quite ill with pancreatic cancer. Her illness came on very quickly. During January 2006 she was admitted to hospital. Her body had started to give up quickly, although her spirit was still feisty. She would have good days and terrible days; obviously the cancer was extremely virulent. She was moved from ward to ward, attended to by young nurses; we watched with great sadness as this 81-year-old woman, with such a lifetime of experiences, became progressively more unwell.

My husband saw that her dignity was gradually ebbing away. It was clear to all that this was an old lady whose youth and life had been forgotten. Paul, as a consequence, found a picture when she was just 16 years old. The picture held the resemblance of the elderly lady, but it portrayed a little twinkle and devilment in those eyes; one we had grown to know and love!

We took the photo into the hospital and showed it to Eva. At first, she didn't take too much notice of it (or so we thought), so we pinned it above her bed. We did this for two reasons: firstly, to show the nurses that Eva was also young once; and secondly, we hoped it would spark Eva off and urge her to recapitulate her life. The second reason soon became true as recapitulate she did... loudly!

Well, she spent the next afternoon and evening relaying her story to anyone who would sit and listen to her! She continually verbalised her life. She was talking and talking! We weren't able to interact in any way, and when we asked her anything at all about the story she was telling she would look back at us with blank eyes... and then carry on with the story and journey of her life.

According to the nurses, Eva was intent on telling her story all through the next night, keeping all of the other patients in the ward awake. During the following week, Eva's spirit was slowly detaching itself from the physical body and she finally died...

Paul and I were honoured to carry out the Death Rites for her. Through held-back tears we conducted the ceremony; being rewarded as we glimpsed the milky essence of her soul leaving her lifeless physical body - going home before beginning its next adventure... wherever that may be.

To Eva: We loved your spirit and we will always love you...

We also learned about the negativity of 'leaving back doors open'. If you imagine your warm cosy home and someone leaves the back door open, all of the warmth in the home escapes outside; a waste of energy.

The same analogy is relevant when we metaphorically *do not* burn our bridges behind us when embarking on a new venture. By leaving our escape doors open, we are fearful that the new venture may fail. This will ensure that our energy becomes misplaced and confused as it is unable to focus on this new venture. Instead it is escaping via the open back door. This will, in turn, hold us within its grip of stagnation, unable to become fully committed to the future.

Here is an example...

Following the completion of my training, I really wanted to become a Shamanic healer.

My old life of crime analyst, even though it paid me a regular wage, was a role that I had trouble now identifying with. This disconnection became so difficult that one day, while analysing burglaries and working out the burglar's profile, I remember drifting off and exploring a possible idea that maybe it is the criminals that need the most help; a radical thought and one that would have caused a serious debate amongst my colleagues and maybe even some of you!

Nevertheless, I began to imagine what a criminal's daily life would entail, especially those that were addicted to drugs (possibly 70% of them). I mulled around the notions of what experiences they had endured in their lives that had driven them along the drugs route. Eventually I came to the conclusion that although I knew that criminality was wrong and dishonourable I could not judge them. I had not experienced what they had experienced. After all I had not even walked a 'mile in their footprints'.

My thoughts led me to realise that we live in a society of success, excess, needs and wants. All of that creates a toxic cocktail of unhappiness and disharmony that humans constantly try to put right. This leaves in its wake a physical body that is weakened, miserable and driven by emotion and emotive behaviours.

I knew that the calling to heal was extremely strong. What could I do about it? I did what most would do and kept a foot in both camps – I provided healing AND I worked as a crime analyst.

This was exhausting. I knew I was not giving my full attention and energy to either, so much so that I started to receive little nudges from spirit. Usually I ignored them. Then I received a hefty nudge, designed to keep me out of action for the next three months.

It happened while I was healing. I had been working on the floor and had to get up and fetch something from my car. Off I trotted out of the front door and as I stepped off the step I felt a painful twang at the back of my knee. The result was a ripped tendon. This gave me plenty of time to think, evaluate and assess my life.

In my heart and etched into my entire being I knew that I was left with no other choice. I simply had to close the back door on the world of crime analyst, giving up a reliable and regular income, and step into the unknown, the world of the healer. Now that was a leap of faith.

Coming to See a Shaman

When a client comes to see a Shaman, they obviously do not go through the same arduous journey around the medicine wheel that we did, as our story is one of wounded healer. A client would expect the Shaman to guide them gently through their healing in a safe and sacred environment. The sessions include joint participation. The Shaman facilitates the healing on the mythic and soul level, and the client undertakes the task of shedding the wounds by agreeing to change the things that no longer serve them on a physical and mental level.

For the healing process to be successful, joint participation is vital. Please do not think that the Shaman is responsible for all of the healing function. Just like those young men who go off into the desert on a quest to find them-selves, you also embark on your own healing and self-realisation quest. How else can one hope to evolve, physically and spiritually?

Your healing journey becomes a search into the unknown and the unknowable. It is a wondrous experiential journey, where you will find out many things about yourself and others. Most of all it is a glimpse of working with the sacred in all things; it is a peek into the world of Living Shamanism, a chance to re-establish ceremony. Even more importantly it becomes the route to authenticity... into the loving arms of your authentic self.

Message from the Author

You may be wondering where you go from here.

Believe me when I say that this is *not* the end of the journey... just the beginning.

When my husband and I finished our training we too felt lost. There was a huge hole left when we left our courses for the last time; we were like birds leaving the nest and unsure of a specific direction to pursue.

The magic that actually follows is unstoppable... this is what happens to *anyone* who signs up to *change* the things that no longer serve them. Our destiny lines realign due to the changes that we are making. The efforts we make to heal, forgive, or to regain the faith that *anything* is possible. Our souls need to move us forward; or to bring in the teachers or healers that we need to further us along our path of ascension... out of the Darkness and into the Light.

The healing journey need not be difficult or arduous. It does not have to be one of constant self atonement or blame for the things that have happened to you or through you. All you need to do is to become aware, change and forgive either yourself or others and heal those wounds.

Simple steps like getting to know who you are from the inside out; accepting *all* aspects of your character that will no longer harm you as you do not hide yourself deep in the shadows of your inner abyss.

Getting to know yourself kicks you out of the closet of self hurt and harm... it offers a spotlight of love and forgiveness.

Don't forget this statement: 'Whatever happens... happens for a reason'. So before you decide where to go next, take a long walk in the warm sunshine or into the woods; or take a bracing stroll on a wet and windy beach.

Re-introduce yourself to Mother Nature again, feel the sun on your back or the wind in your hair... but do go forward with the knowledge that the organising principles of the Universe are out there... to hold your hand, whisper in your ear and support you every step of the way.

Enjoy the journey of self discovery and empowerment!

Munay and blessings

Jules X

Glossary

The Qero, Ayni, Heavy and Light Energy

Here is a brief history of the Qero. This will help you to appreciate some of the principles and teachings which I have either imbibed or which have been awakened from within. It will also help you understand some of the terminology I have used throughout the book.

I must also add that even though I am a practising Shaman, I am not advocating this as the answer for everyone! I purely want to illustrate the importance of having a faith or a path – that which connects you – and what might happen if there is an absence of faith.

Where does one go in order to get help during challenging times? How does one challenge oneself personally in order to promote growth?

Not only is it requisite to have faith in a centred belief system but, equally, we need to have faith in ourselves. We need to feel comfortable in the knowledge that we CAN take responsibility for our own actions, and even more importantly, for the person we have evolved into, for ourselves!

The Qero People from Peru

The Qero people come from Peru and are South American Indians. They live one 183 kilometres from the city of Cusco, located high up in the mountains; the first community you will find here is that of the Quico.

The Nation of Qero is actually made up of eight different communities with over 600 inhabitants. If you track back the history of the Qero, you will find a legend that tells the story of a father who divided his land between his seven sons. Each son, together with their father, cultivated his land and created a community. These eight communities now make up the great

Nation of Qero.

If one were to visit the Qero people, one would have to travel from Cusco by bus for ten hours, then walk for five hours, just to reach the first village; and then an additional four to ten hours to reach any of the outlying villages! It is amazing that all of these villages are located so high up in the mountains, some reaching altitudes of up to 5,500 metres.

The communities within the Qero Nation are generally small. Their houses are still built using a base of stone, granite and straw. The inhabitants have an economy based around the principle activities of agriculture and livestock, as well as creating textiles and weavings using ancient methods.

The Qero people are considered to be the ultimate descendants of the Incas. They have inherited the Inca religion and are guardians of this ancient culture. Even now, you will find that, during the daily lives of the Qero, the Inca customs and traditions have been preserved almost completely intact.

Though many of their traditions and practices are passed on orally, they are still considered to be amongst the best Andean Healers in Peru. As with so many other ancient communities, unfortunately, their children cannot wait to leave the village and head off towards the city in the hope of building a different life for themselves. Inevitably, this means that many of the ancient traditions of their culture are gradually being lost, no longer being passed on from father to son in the old, time-honoured way.

The Qero people maintain a direct relationship with their natural environment, and through this they achieve harmony with the natural world. They believe that they are the 'Children of Mother Earth' and that they are a part of her. Such beliefs awaken in them a deep respect for the things that they consider to be sacred; the mountains, the Earth, the sun, the moon and the lakes. The Qero people have developed their faith through hundreds of years of direct contact with the natural world and with the help and guidance of their Paqo healers.

The Qero practise 'Ayni'… a spiritual law that they live by…

The Meaning of Ayni

'Ayni' is a tradition that teaches harmonious communication with nature as a way of living. It brings the understanding that we are neither separate from, nor above, nature; that we play our part in the intrinsic balance operating throughout the natural world.

With this understanding intact, it becomes possible for humans to connect with what is natural within each one of them also. Once accustomed to thinking in this way, confusion is removed from the human state. It is not only possible, but natural, to connect to the Supreme Consciousness; where we find simple truths and a love disposition which is our own infinite nature. This allows us to live in a state of peace, both within ourselves and within our environment.

Such a state of harmony is epitomised by the sacred law of 'Ayni'; a law taught within the Qero tradition, but essentially one of the most sacred universal laws governing Life itself. 'Ayni', simply put, means reciprocity. It ensures that, by its practice, a social balance will arise within the community. At its core is the act of giving. The sense of honouring which permeates each act of giving is the sole motivator for the giver.

In the Western world, we tend to lean towards a different energy exchange (money); thus: I do something for you and, in return, you pay me for that deed.

The law of 'Ayni' teaches that what has been given is in an energetic form. No matter what the form is, it cannot be kept. We are obliged to give it to another who may be in need at the time.

This law is supported by nature and is obvious in our natural surroundings. A tree does not jealously hold onto its fruits, but gives freely to the insects and the Earth and so on, in abundance. In return, the tree receives what it needs to grow; water, sunlight and minerals from nature. And so the cycle of life perpetuates itself in continuous flow and harmony.

'Ayni' is a determining principle of behaviour and a way of being. In indigenous social structures, 'Ayni' operates as a system of communal, shared labour where, for example, farmers help or work on their neighbours' fields and in return they will receive some of the fruits of their labour.

'Ayni' is also a guiding moral principle, similar to 'do unto others as you would have them do unto you'. In this light, 'Ayni' operates as a moral code; a code of personal conduct.

One can see how it takes on even a greater significance – it is clearly a fundamental, creative principle of the natural world!

The Qero People Recognise Only Two Types of Energy – Sami and Hucha

In this world of living energy that surrounds all things, I would like to take the opportunity to explain a little more about energy...

Our human bodies are surrounded by an energy field, an active electromagnetic field that has the ability to simultaneously emit and absorb vibrations. Vibrations are a wave of frequency in which energy travels.

To help understand a little more, imagine this...

You arrive at work one day, full of the joys of spring! As you walk into the office you are aware that some of your work colleagues seem to be irritated. This has created a heavy mood around the office. Even though the problem isn't anything that you have been involved in, simply by entering the office area, your energy body is exposed to the heavy environment. Very soon you, too, will become affected. Before long, you, too, will experience an irritated and drained feeling.

What has occurred here is an invisible energy exchange. The Qero believe there are basically two types of energy and that we are in a constant state of interchange with them. There is either a heavy, dense energy called Hucha, or a light, refined energy called Sami.

You mediate or juggle these two energy levels through a place within your own energy body called the kawsay poq'po (the energy bubble, or your aura). Your poq'po surrounds and connects with your physical body and you mediate energy through it at a chakra centre located near your navel.

Sami (Light Energy)

The way it works is, in fact, quite simple: Sami saturates the natural world, animating all living beings and imparting power to natural objects and places where it accumulates. The more Sami we incorporate into our own energy body, the more effortlessly and totally we live in harmony and in a state of well-being with others and the natural world. It is by lightening our energy body, by incorporating this vital, refined energy, that we are able to raise our level of consciousness.

Hucha (Heavy Energy)

Hucha, by contrast, is created only by human beings. Hucha manifests because we do not live life in perfect Ayni – reciprocity – with the world of living energy. Hucha results from the way we interact with one another and the natural world, generated by the power of our emotions, thoughts and actions.

Because of the way we tend to be, and the way we tend to live, Hucha cannot be avoided. Therefore, any space which humans have occupied, in which they have lived out their 'humanness', accumulates Hucha.

We can attract Hucha to ourselves simply by walking through a congested city. Most often, however, we accumulate Hucha through our emotional interactions with others. It is generated as we weave our energies amongst those whom we love, hate, envy or nurture. It is an energetic by-product of our pains and sorrows, our fears, our hopes and of the range of feelings that drive our thoughts and actions.

It is a density of energy that we do NOT want to accumulate; it transforms the lightness of our energy body into being heavy like itself. It keeps us from functioning optimally and it prevents us from engaging in the world of living energy as fully as we can. Hucha itself, however, is not negative or bad energy. It is simply heavy or dense. Hucha does not have a moral code. You could even think of it as an organised energy that becomes disorganised.

Unfortunately, in the West, we are always trying to reduce everything to positive or negative; good or bad; right or wrong. But heaviness is a relative thing. It is the fruit of our accumulation of heavy energy that manifests in ways that we tend to think of as negative. When we are not in peak energetic form, then we tend not to experience full physical, mental, or emotional well-being. Instead we become 'un-harmonious', diseased or 'ill at ease' with ourselves and our surroundings. So much so, we become disconnected from the natural flow of nature's energies and we lose our rightful place in this world.

From a psychological perspective, Hucha can be seen as the accumulation in our energy body of all that does not serve us. For example negative attitudes, untruthfulness, the inability to love. We may even become self-destructive or hurtful to others.

Maybe, as you read this, you realise that you are experiencing some of these conditions right now. In that case, you are probably under the influence of an energy that is heavy – Hucha is manifesting itself somewhere in your life. Heaviness, however, is relative to each individual and the condition of their own particular energy field. Heaviness indicates an incompatibility between personal energy and an external energy.

Fear, for example, is an indication that you are in contact with something that is heavy for you. Incompatible types of energy feel heavy, but heaviness is a relative thing. What is heavy for you may not be heavy for me!

Understanding energy as heavy as opposed to negative is

crucial as this perceptual shift is imperative to living fully and consciously, open and receptive to the energies of others and the natural world.

For example: If you come across energy that you perceive as negative, your only course of action, or likely course of action, is to *protect* yourself! However, in doing so, you close yourself off and risk turning your energy body into an 'energetic jail' or placing barriers around yourself. However, if instead you become *aware* of this incompatibility, your awareness will allow you then to act on it and actually transform the energy, in effect, lighten it. You do this so that it either becomes compatible for you or simply does not affect you.

At such times, even if you cannot deal with the Hucha completely, and it seems too much for you to handle all at once, it presents NO danger to you, and there is no need to close off your energy body in the impulse toward protection, because, in and of itself, the Hucha has no capacity to harm you!

For further information and reading, I would recommend: *Masters of the Living Energy* by Joan Parisi Wilcox.

Shamanic Practitioners... Feeling Safe
Using the services of a Shaman may be a relatively new experience for many of you. It may even be something that you have never considered before. I know that many have already visited complementary therapists such as acupuncturists, homoeopathists, osteopaths or Reiki therapists, but very few have visited a Shaman.

What Should I Look for?
When seeking out the services of a Shaman, do look for one that has been trained by a reputable organisation, preferably one who offers a range of services, ensuring that you undergo the best possible care in a structured and safe format.

For example, some people may go to a Shaman purely for a

soul retrieval (a soul retrieval returns a part of the soul that has left the physical body, either under duress or after a bad experience) and all they will receive is just that treatment.

It is my view, however, that if one brings a soul part back to an energy field that has not undergone energy clearing first (cleaning the energy body of any wounds that may have been responsible for the soul part leaving in the first place), a soul retrieval purely on its own may *not* always be the best healing to carry out, as the soul part may well leave again.

In the Shamanic traditions that we have been taught, we firstly make sure that we clear the imprints of dis-ease, and only then will we carry out soul retrieval if we feel it is necessary.

Please also make sure that your Shaman offers you after care. This should take the form of a follow-up consultation, thus ensuring that your progress is assessed before any further follow-up sessions. By doing this, the layers of toxic energy are gently and gradually removed, possibly allowing other issues to rise to the surface.

You should also have the opportunity to telephone or email your Shaman should you feel unwell or worried after receiving any treatments. It is also imperative that you feel safe with your chosen Shaman. If you feel scared or worried while in their company DO NOT go through with the consultation. Your own sense of well-being is *always* the best guide!

Make sure that it is not *you* driving the session, for example by saying: 'I need soul retrieval'. Your Shaman should guide your healing as they have been trained to do so, not the other way around.

During your first Shamanic session, your Shaman should explain to you what is going to happen, approximately how long the sessions will run, and how many you could expect to receive (although the timing is not a precise science).

For example, if you go to a Shaman for a quick fix then it is *not* going to be successful. If you have carried the imprint of the wound for 15 years or so, then you may well expect to receive between four and six sessions, sometimes more, before you feel in harmony with yourself again.

Make sure that you know *exactly* the cost of each session. Will it be an hourly charge or a cost for all sessions? You should also expect to be given a consultation where the Shaman takes down your full case history.

You should expect to be treated in a clean environment. You should expect your consultation to be confidential. You should also expect to remain fully clothed at all times with the very minimum of any personal contact.

However, you should be aware that you and the Shaman will be working close to each other, but without touching.

A Shamanic session usually lasts anywhere between one and two hours.

To give you some idea of the extensive range of Shamanic services that you can expect to receive from a Four Winds Graduate, see below:

- Energy clearing of imprints left from wounds, issues and events that have proved to be toxic in your life.
- Crystallised and/or Entity Extractions.
- Soul Retrieval.
- Destiny Retrieval.
- Despacho Ceremonies
- The Munay Ki Rites.
- Rites of Passage*.
- The Death Rites.
- Personal development opportunities to back-up the healing sessions.
  *Offered by some Shamanic practitioners.

Shamanic processes, even though often based on ancient healing methods, are eminently successful for treating the effects of modern day living. They may be used to remove the imprints or toxic sludge of wounds, events and issues that have caused disease within you or your family.

A Shaman can work with your energy field to remove the imprints that are causing physical or mental problems. He/she can travel to the 'Otherworlds' to facilitate your healing. They can also conduct healing for ancestors or loved ones that have passed away in an unhealed state.

The healing processes work at a deep level and can occasionally bring up other hidden issues from the depths – these also need healing.

Some sessions require that you undergo some personal developmental issues. These usually come in the form of awareness, recognition, acceptance and a willingness to change something that no longer serves you.

Remember: 'If you change nothing, nothing changes'.

Some of these adjustments may also involve life-style changes. If you do not take your healing seriously then spirit will not be convinced that you are serious enough to make yourself well again!

About the Author

Julie has been a practising Shaman since 2005. With her husband Paul they created a resource website www.4directions.co.uk to help introduce Peruvian Samanic healing into our Western society. They felt it was important to de-mystify the various healing modalities. This website clarifies each healing modality that Four Winds' trained graduates offer around the world.

There is also a 'Where to Find Us' section on the website, listing graduates that offer Peruvian Healing around the globe.

During the same year Ayni Shamans Shop was formed. This was the first Peruvian Textile and Shamanic Tools site in the UK and Europe; sourcing textiles, incenses and ceremonial tools from both the Qero and Shipibo Tribes.

Julie opened the first high street Shamanic healing clinic in 2007, bringing Shamanic healing out of the closet into the open. This clinic proved to be very successful once again, by removing the mystery of shamanic healing.

Julie currently runs her own Shamanic Healing Clinic in County Wexford, Southern Ireland. You can visit her website at www.aynishamnichealing.eu. She integrates all core Peruvian Shamanic healing processes into her work with clients that come from far reaches to see her. She also offers intensive training and healing days over two, three or four days.

Julie is happy to discuss any of the different processes with you. She also offers one-on-one or small-group Shamanic Lifestyle Training.

Resources

If you would like to find out more about Shamanic services and the locations of a selection of Four Winds' trained professionals, please visit:

www.4directions.co.uk

To contact the author for Shamanic healing, then visit her website:

www.aynishamanichealing.eu

If you are interested in purchasing or sourcing Peruvian textiles or Shamanic ceremonial tools, please go to:

www.aynishamansshop.co.uk

Recommended Reading

Masters of the Living Energy, the Mystical World of the Q'ero People by Joan Parisi Wilcox 2004.

Dance of the Four Winds – by Alberto Villoldo & Erik Jendresen 1995

Shaman Healer Sage – by Alberto Villoldo 2001

Mending the Past & Healing the Future – by Alberto Villoldo 2005

The Four Insights – by Alberto Villoldo 2006

Radical Forgiveness – by Colin Tipping 2010

Divine Magic – by Doreen Virtue 2006

The Celestine Prophecy – by James Redfield 1994

She – by Robert A Johnson 1989

He – by Robert A Johnson 1991

The Dark Side of the Light Chasers – by Debbie Ford 2001

The Secret Places of the Burren – by John M Feehan 1986

Eminent Lives – by Francis Crick 2011

Many Lives, Many Masters – by Dr Brian Weiss 1994

A Spiral of Memory and Belonging – by Frank Henderson MacEowen 2004

Shamanic Experience – by Kenneth Meadows 2001

Galdrbok, Practical Heathen Runecraft, Shamanism & Magic – by Nathan Johnson & Robert J Wallis 2005

Soul Retrieval, Mending the Fragmented Self – by Sandra Ingerman 2010

The World Is As You Dream it – by John Perkins 1994

Shapeshifting Techniques for Global and Personal Transformations – by John Perkins 1999

The Alchemy of Sacred Living – by Emory John Michael 1998

MOON

BOOKS

Moon Books invites you to begin or deepen your encounter with Paganism, in all its rich, creative, flourishing forms.